well at oailleville –

SUFFOLK

VISION OF ENGLAND

General Editors, Clough and Amabel Williams-Ellis

SUFFOLK

OLIVE COOK

drawings and water-colours by Rowland Suddaby

PAUL ELEK LONDON

Published in 1948 by
PAUL ELEK PUBLISHERS LTD
38 Hatton Garden, London E.C.1
Printed by W S Cowell Ltd, Ipswich
Photographs selected by Sarah Clutton
Jacket and cover designed by Kenneth Rowntree
Layout and Typography by Peter Ray, F.S.I.A.

The figures on the cover are
Edward Fitzgerald and John Constable

The frontispiece drawing is
Cornfields and the River Stour, Sudbury

Catalogue No. 196/9

CONTENTS

1. FIRST IMPRESSIONS
page 7

2. HISTORIC NAMES AND PLACES
page 12

3. THE SENSE OF THE PAST
page 18

4. THE CHURCHES
page 22

5. THE HOME OF THE FLINT KNAPPERS
page 30

6. THE RIVERS
page 32

7. THE COAST
page 38

8. THE PAINTING OF SUFFOLK
page 41

9. SOME LITERARY ASSOCIATIONS
page 46

10. EPILOGUE
page 54

INDEX
page 55

ILLUSTRATIONS
page 57

MAP
facing page 88

FIRST IMPRESSIONS

THE farthest east of England is commonly known as Silly Suffolk. The adjective, like the countryside itself, has a significance not at first apparent: the opening words of an epitaph on the tomb of Sir Thomas Glemham of Little Glemham reveal its original meaning, blest:

This sylly grave the happy cynders hyde . . .

The expression of seeming ridicule thus becomes an apt description of this shy, solitary county where there is one church to every six hundred inhabitants and where it is impossible to spend half a day without becoming aware of a deep, strange sense of peace. The quiet villages and old market towns with their pargeted and half timbered houses seem lost in a dream which has been unbroken for generations; the narrow, winding lanes where the light itself becomes green as it filters through the thick leaves of summer, know nothing of the motorist.

Motorists usually travel through Suffolk along the main roads and I have often heard them dismiss the county as flat and uninteresting. It is indeed without the obvious drama of mountain, rock and waterfall, but the scattered, irregular villages, the great churches, the manor houses, the farms and simple cottages of Suffolk are set in a landscape of refreshing richness and variety, a landscape of sea, meadow, moor and marsh. The gentle hills disclose vistas of unexpected splendour, great lonely expanses of field and wood. The haphazard woods springing up all over Suffolk give delightful diversity to the country without overriding it. They are mostly of oak. The dizzy yellow of the leaves in April is a shining foil to the bare fields, but in winter the oaks make a brown mass, sparkling when the light falls across them, black and menacing in shadow, standing out even on the far distant horizon with more force and darkness than anything close at hand. The Suffolk woods are nevertheless gentle in spirit, airy and full of flowers; large white or deep purple violets grow there, they burst with pale starry anemones and primroses, then with bluebells and red campion. Only the Druidic Forest near Butley is gloomy, alien and almost flowerless. The trees, some of them gigantic in size, are the once sacred oak, ash and holly and they grow so closely together that on the brightest day the light is obscured, the atmosphere eerie and oppressive.

Little streams and rivers run all over Suffolk. There are so many of them besides the principal waterways—the Stour, the Orwell, the Deben and the Waveney—that it is impossible to know or to name them all. Among them are the Lark and the Linnet, the Glem and the Box, the Dove and the Alde and the Minsmere, each with its own personality, each enriching the landscape with luxuriant watermeadows and mint-fragrant reaches. Above the brilliant green which marks the course of these rivulets slope immense, undulating cornfields. In the west they are separated by low, almost invisible hedges or by none at all, but in the heart of Suffolk and towards the coast they are more often enclosed by high, rioting hedges overgrown with dog-roses and honeysuckle, entangled in a profusion of cowparsley, loosestrife and meadowsweet.

The pink or cream-coloured farms and cottages sometimes stand deep in grass far from the road, the churches often rise isolated in the landscape, approached by no more than rough tracks. A muddy lane announces the church at Alpheton which lies in a smooth meadow close by a cow barn. Loose hay blows among the gravestones and a dank pond stagnates beneath the church tower. Round towered Frostenden crowns a low hill at the end of a narrow footpath and shares a gate with a farmyard. Red and pink outbuildings lean towards the church and behind a screen of elms a yellow Georgian farmhouse with blue pilasters at its door can be seen. On every side stretch the rolling fields, the air is fresh with the smell of the sea and full of butterflies—walls, meadow-browns and large heaths.

Apart from the churches the most distinctive buildings in the Suffolk landscape are the old manor houses in their romantic parks. There is scarcely a village without its hall or great house. Kentwell Hall, near Long Melford, is a small but exquisite example. The dark red Elizabethan house with its domed turrets is perfectly reflected in the calm, encircling water of the broad moat. It is embowered in trees, massive cedars, elms and oaks and it is approached by a remarkable avenue of limes, more than a mile long and entirely straight. On a June evening the avenue is a place of enchantment. The mysterious scent of the limes, the cry of the owls, the pale gleam of the park seen through the tree trunks, the gathering obscurity and the single illuminated window at the distant end of the walk quicken the dullest imagination. Hengrave Hall, near Bury St. Edmunds, is more celebrated and of a more striking beauty. This silver-grey house, fantastically crowded with pinnacles and domes, is best seen on a dull morning. Then it starts from its background of sombre firs with the luminosity of a vision. Before the house, close cut lawns and clipped yews are bordered by trim, precise ranks of dwarf limes. Beyond, an ornamental gate leads into a vast park where sheep graze. To the right of the house a tiny chapel with a round Norman tower stands clustered about by yews near the edge of a lake. The air is moist, the soft call of the woodpigeon only accentuates the profound stillness of the place. The lake is overgrown, a boat slowly rots where it is moored and in the chapel sleep the great families who lived and made their home at Hengrave, the Darcys, the Bouchiers, the Gages and the Kytsons. Mockbeggar Hall in the parish of Claydon is as impressive, though for quite other reasons. Its builders and first owners have left no trace behind them. It is a gabled Elizabethan house of the grimmest aspect. The origin of its strange name is given by Green in his *Short History of the English People*:

At the close of Elizabeth's reign and throughout the reign of James I and the early years of Charles, there was much complaining in the rural districts because the nobles and gentry flocked up to London, leaving their country houses empty and neglected so that where in former times there had been feasting for rich and poor alike a beggar could not now get a crust of bread. To the houses thus deserted was given the nickname of Mockbeggar Hall.

About this house, though it now seems to be well cared for, there is an inexpressible atmosphere of desolation and menace. Once seen, its image will always haunt the mind.

All these houses take their place naturally in the Suffolk scene and contribute to the peculiar spirit of the countryside. There is another seat whose astonishing shape and size will not be denied a part in any description of Suffolk though it has no affinity with the soil on which it stands and would engrave itself with equal force upon the memory whatever spot in England had been chosen as its site. The vast stucco oval of Ickworth in the neighbourhood of Bury is the work of a remarkable and eccentric man who never saw it erected nor its first stone laid. He was the fourth Earl of Bristol, Bishop of Derry, the strangest and most intriguing of that family whose oddities gave rise to the witticism that the world was composed of men, women and Herveys. The great Folly house was begun in 1792 and when the Bishop died in 1803, in Italy, it needed but the stairway and minor details to complete it; these were added by the fifth Earl in 1826. A raised terrace on the south boundary of the garden yields a striking view of the house. Above shaven lawns and thick box borders, above a sea of exotic evergreens, even above its background of gigantic cedars towers the rotunda, one hundred and five

Farm near Bury St. Edmunds

feet high. It has a double row of Ionic columns carrying heavy entablatures and the upper part of the dome is ornamented by a frieze of bas-reliefs copied by two Milanese brothers from Flaxman's designs of subjects from the *Iliad* and the *Odyssey*. On either side the rotunda is connected by curving corridors to many-windowed wings. It was the Bishop's plan to confine the domestic apartments of the house to the rotunda and to devote corridors and wings to the display of works of art. And although the collection he was making for Ickworth was incomplete at the time of his death it includes pictures by Gainsborough, Zoffany, Reynolds, Hogarth and Velazquez and the portrait of the owner by Angelica Kauffmann with whom he consorted in Rome.

Boxted, small, unfrequented and un-famed, may serve as an example, chosen because of my long familiarity with the scene, of the rich pastoral beauty of the Suffolk parks. The Hall, a half timbered Elizabethan house, does not stir the fancy like Kentwell, Hengrave or Mockbeggar Hall, but it lies low and from the back is almost invisible behind high trees. It is from the back, from the road that runs to Hawkedon, that the park is best approached. A modest white gate opens upon a broad path gently rising and slowly curving round to the unseen house. It is bordered by widely spaced pines and oaks. To the right a bank slopes from a hedge of hollies. From the top of this bank, where the fine grass is strewn with acorn cups and the air is sweet with the smell of the pines, a romantic landscape unfolds itself. An enormous ploughed field, a deep purple against the embracing green, ends far away in the dark fir copse which hides the house. Above the trees, through a tracery of light green leaves Boxted Church can be seen on the top of a hill. Towards the left the field gives way to brilliant meadow lands, studded with clumps of firs, shaggy oaks and naked, blasted trunks. The river Glem with willows on its farther bank runs through the meadows and the rising ground beyond is crowned by an oak wood. On the hillside a white horse crops.

Placid as it must appear on first acquaintance, Suffolk has its dramatic moments. Cobbett remarked on the brightness of the atmosphere in East Anglia. The light there has a vibrating, electric quality which, especially in spring, charges the landscape with a feeling of intensity. Then large, garish clouds, heavy with rain or hail, sweep the countryside with their broad shadows; the great churches are images of silver against the darkness, the vivid greens and yellows of the young foliage dazzle the eye. The common sight of the Suffolk Punches drawing the harrow across a flat brown field with the red roofs of a village half concealed by tall trees in the background is momentarily transformed by the glitter of the light into something strange and significant. The glossy chestnut coats of the horses, the great aprons of cloud, the front of a row of pink cottages suddenly receive the full force of the blinding light while the trees and houses behind become dense, threatening masses of shadow. It is as spectacular as a violent storm in other districts, though it endures for but an instant, relaxing almost immediately into the charming light and shade of an ordinary bright spring day.

The peacefulness of the Suffolk countryside is counterbalanced not only by the dramatic play of light but by the wildness of the sea and the tragic story of the coast. All along the low shores of sand and shingle folk tell of the sea's siege and of the towns and villages the sea has won. It is a wasted land where history is waiting to repeat itself in sad stories for people yet unborn. When the Romans colonised England they built near Felixstowe a camp as great as Burgh Castle, but today there remains no trace of it, for the breakers roll shorewards over its site; Dunwich, once the see of a bishopric, lies beneath the waves; a little of Pakefield succumbs with every winter gale; the old Moot Hall of Aldeburgh, formerly the centre of the town, now stands on the beach, awaiting the encroaching tide.

There are but four sizeable towns in Suffolk: Ipswich, Bury, Felixstowe and Lowestoft, and except for Bury they contribute little to the essential spirit of Suffolk as I know it. Ipswich, the capital of the county, must once have been an enchanting place, but today it has all been engulfed by straggling outskirts, characterless modern villas and council houses. Even in the centre much of Ipswich has been rebuilt; the monasteries have vanished, the old timbered houses have been pulled down, the musty, crooked taverns demolished. Almost the only relics of other days are the famous Great White Horse Inn where Mr Pickwick had his disconcerting experience with the 'lady in yellow curl papers', Wolsey's Gate and the extraordinary Elizabethan building at the corner of St. Stephen's Lane known as the Ancient House. The basement front is of oak panelling embellished with carved leaves and flowers; above are five huge bay windows with plaster figures in relief on their bases. One of these is clearly Atlas sinking beneath the weight of his globe. The others are a woman with a camel's head by her side, an ample lady holding a sceptre and a cornucopia, a figure with a bow and arrow and a woman riding upon a crocodile. According to inscriptions they represent Asia, Europe, America and Africa. Wolsey's Gate in College Street is a simple brick archway bearing the arms of Henry VIII. It is all that remains of a great college, which once extended over six acres

Opposite. Church and Barn, Stoke-by-Nayland

of ground, and which Cardinal Wolsey began to build two years before disgrace fell upon him in 1530. He had intended it to furnish scholars for his even greater college of Christ Church, Oxford. Wolsey was an Ipswich boy, the son of a butcher, according to tradition, though recent authorities believe his father to have been a well-to-do grazier.

Unlike the rest of the town the atmosphere of the docks has hardly changed since Gainsborough made his delicate pencil sketches of Ipswich sailing ships and men busy at the quayside. Gigantic cranes and steamships now occupy the foreground of the scene, but seamen come and go or stand and stare towards the mouth of the Orwell, bright sails skim over the broad, placid water and on the far bank the pleasant parks, meadows and woods of Suffolk stretch away to the low horizon as they did two centuries ago.

The Suffolk people are soft spoken and kindly, though like all East Anglians reserved and sometimes uncomfortably independent. 'There never was suthen for nuthen, nor I don't suppose there ever will be,' a farm labourer once said, and his attitude is general in Suffolk. I once made a present of fruit to a neighbour and was immediately asked 'How much is it?' Nor would she rest easy until she had given a similar present in return. The country speech, a low sing-song, has in the remoter districts a liveliness and a full flavour which have never been contaminated by urban influences and which even the radio has failed to spoil, though few cottages are without it. A girl is still a 'mawther' in Suffolk, dew is 'dag', a dark night is 'black as iron'. Wheat that is long in the straw is 'all flushed up to nuthen', fallen apples must not lie too long or they will all go 'clung'. My grandmother, who lived in Wickhambrook, on one occasion dismissed a smart new dress thus: 'How yeow dew go flacketen about.' And she had constantly to admonish us children with the threat, 'I'll gi ye such a ding i' the hid 'a ye dew so no more.'

The Suffolk sense of ridicule is as dis-tinctive as the language. The story of the labourer and the passing motorist is typical. 'Do you know the time?' asked the motorist. After struggling for some minutes to extract his watch from the top pocket of his corduroys the labourer looked at it carefully, then replied, 'Yes, thank God I dew', replaced the timepiece and continued his work. The following epitaph is an example of the grim, fatalistic character which East Anglian humour can sometimes assume:

> She once the fairest flower of May
> Now turned to lifeless clay.
> Good God, what can we say?

2

HISTORIC NAMES AND PLACES

FROM the banks of Breydon Water, the estuary of the Yare and the Waveney, the impressive bulk of Burgh Castle throws a shadow that chills the warmth of summer and spreads over cornfield and thicket. The Castle is a relic of the Roman Occupation with which the history of Suffolk begins. Though corn grows now where Cæsar's legions fought and feasted, the great walls and massive round bastions confront the landscape as boldly and triumphantly as when they were first built nineteen hundred years ago.

The Romans have left traces of their presence all over the county. Archeologists frequently find the remains of villas, pots, coins and sepulchral urns, but some of the most startling discoveries have been made by the people themselves. A large bronze Venus was turned up by the plough at Wenhaston and a statuette of Nero at Barking. At West Row, near Mildenhall, as recently as 1946, a farm labourer stumbled upon the remarkable treasure now exhibited at the British Museum, Roman trays, dishes, goblets, finger bowls and spoons, all of silver.

The Angles, who came across the North Sea, probably settled in Suffolk during the last half of the fifth century. Redwald was the first king of East Anglia to accept Christianity, though his acceptance must have been half-hearted, for according to Bede, 'he set up in the same temple an altar for the Christian sacrifice and one for offerings to devils'. And if Redwald was the king whose burial ship was unearthed at Sutton Hoo not far from Woodbridge he must have eventually reverted to the faith of his fathers. The timbers of this great barge had crumbled away, but its shape was impressed upon the sandy soil, and the eight-inch iron nails which had once secured the planks to the ribs were still in position. The sight of the treasure with which the ship was heaped, personal ornaments, weapons, gold, precious stones, spoons, bowls and drinking horns instantly revives that unreal period, thirteen centuries ago, when Redwald ruled the kingdom of East Anglia. All that the king valued in life, all that he might need to journey to an unknown land and to defend himself against unseen foes, were placed in the barge. An iron sword enriched with gold and with garnets, a shield with a great bronze boss wrought with the heads of fabulous monsters, an iron helmet adorned with a face of bronze, an axe, spearheads, javelins and a carved whetstone lay cheek by jowl with buckles of pure gold, strappings of gold studded with garnets, golden plaques, coins and purses. Two huge armlets suggest that the wearer was of gigantic stature. Whoever he was, this king was among the last to be buried with such splendour, for by the seventh century St. Cedd and St. Felix had come to Suffolk to preach the gospel of a future awakening where neither treasures would be needed for consolation nor earthly weapons for protection.

During Saxon times Suffolk was continually harassed by the Danes. It was on the occasion of a Scandinavian raid that King Edmund met his tragic end. Edmund was born about 841 and was crowned King of East Anglia when he was only a boy of fifteen. The ceremony took place at Bures, on Christmas Day, in a little church where the old thatched building known as Chapel Barn now stands. By paying tribute to the Danes, Edmund hoped to reign in peace; but in vain. The enemy burst into his kingdom and overwhelmed his forces at Hoxne. Legend relates that the king escaped and, exhausted, sought refuge beneath Goldbrook Bridge. The Danes, it is said, lost track of him, but a bride and bridegroom on their way to church dallied on the bridge and by chance caught sight of Edmund's golden spurs as he lay sleeping. They immediately disclosed his hiding place. The Danes seized him, bade him surrender half his treasure, renounce his faith and reign as a vassal. When Edmund refused, the heathen bound him to a tree, scourged him, riddled him with arrows and beheaded him. As he died, Edmund cursed all young men and maids who should ever cross Goldbrook Bridge and no wedding party has ever dared to take that path since.

For thirty-three years the martyr lay at Hoxne. Then it was decided to remove the body to a shrine at Bury where a monastery known as Beodricsworth had been established as far back as 637. But the king's head could not be found. For forty days the searchers scoured the countryside and they had almost lost hope when suddenly in the heart of a forest they heard a voice crying, 'Here, here, here,'

And never ceased of all that longe day
So for to cry tyl they cam where he lay.

And they found the head miraculously preserved and guarded by a monstrous wolf who was holding the sacred object between his paws. The head and body thus brought together were instantly united so that the mark of the union was scarcely visible. The crest of Bury St. Edmund's for this reason bears on it a wolf sitting and offering the crowned head of St. Edmund between his paws. The great oak beneath which the king was done to death is supposed to have stood until the middle of the last century when it crashed in a summer storm. But a Suffolk resident writing in the *Gentleman's Magazine* in 1848, the year when the oak fell, denies on the strength of fifty years' knowledge of the district, that the tree was traditionally connected with the martyrdom. Be that as it may, the head of an ancient arrow was found embedded in the trunk of the oak and it has been preserved at Hengrave Hall as a relic of St. Edmund.

Pilgrims came from far and wide to pray at Edmund's shrine at Bury. Many stories are told of its miraculous powers. The sick and the lame were healed and on one occasion intending robbers were shackled by the saint in the Abbey until the officers of justice came to take them. A man was struck blind for attempting to view the incorruptible corpse but his sight was restored after repentance. So great was the sanctity of the martyr's body that King Sweyn is said to have been punished by death because he demanded exhorbitant taxes of St. Edmund's people. Once a young monk tried to pull at the arms and feet of the body to prove its incorruptibility, but in the words of an old chronicler 'contracted were his nerves for ever after'. It was before St. Edmund's shrine that the barons met to swear that King John should do their will and sign Magna Carta.

Long before this, Bury had become the most important town in East Anglia and several parliaments were held there. It is the modern capital of West Suffolk, but it lives on its memories of medieval greatness. There is a greyness, an air of melancholy about it which are only emphasised by the few modern stores and cinemas. Except on market days the narrow streets are often quite silent and empty; even Angel Hill is usually deserted but for the visitors come to view the remains of antiquity. The square towering Norman gateway to the Abbey is one of the most moving sights in all England. Its great size and the beauty of its proportions cannot be adequately conveyed in a photograph. On every side are three tiers of arcades, all richly decorated with geometrical designs. Strange gargoyles like salamanders coil from the top of two of the walls. Within the archway, round which runs a giant cable ornament, the worn traces of Romanesque carvings can be seen, men and horses with large sloping eyes, spiralling hair, and drapery and trappings arranged in patterned whorls. This remarkable building is railed in and chained up so that it can have no part in the life of Bury today. No one may pass beneath that great arch, no bicycle may lean against those immense walls. The tower is an exhibition piece, a ghost of past glory.

The Abbey Gateway, Bury St. Edmunds

The fourteenth-century gateway which stands close by the Norman tower is still in use. It is of a mellow grey-green colour and it has slender clustered shafts, lively carvings, canopied niches and traceried panels. Once it was the main entrance to the richest Benedictine monastery in the whole country; now it leads to a pleasure garden of green turf divided by an ancient wall from the River Lark. A few shapeless, decaying fragments of masonry are all that survive of crypt, chapel, kitchens, cellars, mint, almonry, refectory and Abbot's Palace. Where the monks worked and prayed, where Jocelyn of Brakelond chronicled the doings of the famous Abbot Samson, where John Lydgate wrote his unreadable narrative poems, lovers now sit and unruly children scream and play.

Among those of William the Conquerors' followers to receive grants of land in Suffolk was the turbulent family of Bigod, whose memory is associated with the castles of Bungay and Framlingham. Hugh Bigod played a prominent part in the wars of the barons and was conspicuous for his treachery, boldness and rapacity. It was he who, having made his stronghold at Bungay almost impregnable, boasted in the time of King Stephen:

> Were I in my Castle of Bungaye
> Above the Water of Waveneye
> I would not care for the King of Cockneye
> And all his meiny.

Later Hugh housed the unprincipled Earl of Leicester and an army of Flemings at Framlingham, and inciting the Princes to rebellion, tried conclusions with Henry II at Fornham St. Genevieve. The insurrection failed and both Framlingham and Bungay were dismantled as a punishment of Hugh Bigod's offence. Something of the personality of the swashbuckling castellan still clings about the ruins overlooking the little town of Bungay. The castle seems toy-like in size but the thick broken walls are full of defiance. They are built upon the isthmus at the base of Suffolk's far flung peninsular of Outney. Beneath the Castle the ground slopes away abruptly to the river and the impenetrable marshes so that Bigod's stronghold is a natural fortress, accessible only from the mainland.

Framlingham was restored after Hugh Bigod's death, by his son Roger. In the reign of Edward I it reverted to the Crown and came eventually into the possession of the Howards, who created the splendid exterior we see today. Framlingham, a ghostly old town of narrow streets, pink and white cottages, a great church and a tiny market place, is dominated by the castle. It rests on high ground above the River Alde, which is here no more than a stream. The battlemented walls, crowned by thirteen towers, rise up out of a vast green moat, surrounded by trees that seem twice as high as trees could ever be, and approached by trim lawns. From every point of view the walls appear entire. There is no suggestion of ruin, no shattered masonry, no crumbling piles of mortar, no clutching ivy. It is something of a shock to enter the court and find that this castle, so perfect in outline, is but a shell. Within the shell stands a group of gabled buildings constructed in the seventeenth century in accordance with an extraordinary will. Sir Robert Hitcham, a lawyer to whom the Howards had sold the castle, directed that on his death the whole interior of Framlingham was to be pulled down and the material used to build almshouses.

Thomas Howard led the English army to victory at Flodden Field and when he died in 1524 his body was borne with pomp from Framlingham to Thetford. But of all the Howards the most sympathetic character is Henry, who is known in literature as the Earl of Surrey. His name is linked with that of Wyatt, and though his verse is conventional in feeling it has lyrical grace and freshness. Gifted and chivalrous, Henry Howard was also hot-tempered and reckless, 'the most foolish proud boy that is in England'. Once he rashly set about magnifying the lineage of the Howards. He boasted of their supposed descent from Edward the Confessor and even attempted to quarter the royal arms with his own on the family shield. He was clapped into the Tower, tried on the flimsiest evidence and beheaded at Tower Hill. The tomb of Henry Howard and his wife is the finest in Framlingham church. Of painted alabaster, the two figures lie upon embroidered pillows with closed eyes and hands clasped in prayer. Both are dressed in fur-bordered cloaks. Henry wears armour; there is a coronet by his head and a great seal hangs about his neck. At either end of the tomb kneel his two sons and his two daughters.

Perhaps the most dramatic moment in the history of Framlingham was the visit of Bloody Mary in 1533. She arrived a fugitive and left a queen. When the news of Edward VI's death reached her, Mary was at Hunsdon. Acting on the advice of her staunchest supporters, Jermingham and Bedingfield, she put on the guise of an old market woman and went immediately to Framlingham, a place from which she could soon reach the coast should she be forced to flee from England. Her standard was hardly hoisted at the gate tower before the Suffolk knights came flocking to join her, among them Cornwallis, Drury, Tyrrel and Shelborn. From that time until she entered London all went well with her. Mary left behind her at Framlingham such plenty of provisions that a barrel of beer was sold for sixpence and four great loaves for a penny. Yet unsavoury tales were told of this visit after her death. The people of Framlingham declared that she had given birth in the Castle to a horrible, half-human monster, whose brains she had dashed out against the stone walls of her room.

During Mary's satanic reign thirty-six persons died at the stake in Suffolk. The most notable of them was Dr. Rowland Taylor. A distinguished Cambridge scholar, he was educated as a Catholic, but the preaching of Hugh Latimer started a doubt in his mind and he became a Protestant and chaplain to Cranmer. Cranmer appointed him to Hadleigh, where he was the best loved pastor in all Suffolk. One day, after Mary Tudor had begun her persecutions, Taylor heard the bell of his church ringing when the building should have been closed. He hastened there to find a strange Catholic priest celebrating mass. When he protested he was thrust out of the church, the door was locked in his face and the Lord High Chancellor was informed that he had tried to prohibit the mass. Bishop Gardiner, like the wretched Dowsing, the Hammer of the Protestants, was a Suffolk man, and one of the most sinister figures in English history. It was he who framed the Six Articles which made it possible to burn a woman alive for denying the humanity of Christ, a man for denying His divinity, and anyone for eating meat on a Friday. Gardiner ordered that Rowland Taylor should be stripped and the robes of a Roman Catholic priest put forcibly upon him. Then he was sentenced to death.

He began his last journey in the depths of night, followed through the dark, shrouded streets of Hadleigh by his weeping wife and little children. When they came to Aldham Common, where the stake was prepared, Taylor said, 'Thanked be God, I am even at home'. He gave away his clothes to those about him and had begun to preach to his loyal parishioners when he was silenced by a heavy blow from one of his escort. Ordered to set light to the pyre, one of the villagers pretended to lameness, but others soon showed their willingness. The martyr stepped into the pitch barrel and was chained to the stake. As the flames leapt up he prayed in a firm voice and with his hands folded across his breast he submitted to the fire.

Queen Elizabeth was a frequent visitor to Suffolk. She is said to have rested beneath the famous Bramfield Oak, of which no more than a stump remains today; she spent delightful days at Hawstead Place, now a farmhouse; she was godmother to one of the Tollemaches of Helmingham and performed there upon the flute. She stayed at Christchurch Mansion, Ipswich, now a museum; she was entertained at Rougham, Shelly and at Smallbridge Hall, near Bures. She held her court in the drawing room of Rushbrooke Hall in 1578; the hangings of the bed in which she slept are tangible reminders of her visit, which is further commemorated by a clock bell over the main porch and three stone heads of the Queen herself. Sir William Cordell feasted her at Long Melford and she called on her cousin Baron Hunsdon at Huntingfield, where a bowed and broken old oak marks the spot on which she stood to shoot the deer.

All the Stuart kings found their way to Newmarket. James I built the King's House and hunted along the ancient earthwork known as the Devil's Dyke and over the wilderness of Breckland. Charles I was painted here by Van Dyck, and Charles II started a horserace which is still run today.

Opposite. Quay on the Deben, Woodbridg

Glimpses of the licence of his carousals at Newmarket are given by Pepys and by Evelyn, who seems to have been extremely ill at ease in the sporting town with the 'jolly blades racing, dauncing, feasting and revelling, more resembling a luxurious and abandon'd rout'.

During Charles II's reign two great naval battles between the English and the Dutch were fought off the Suffolk coast, the first near Lowestoft on June 3rd, 1665, and the second off Southwold on May 28th, 1672. In the battle of 1665 the Dutch were defeated by two Lowestoft admirals, Allen and Utber. The second engagement was the celebrated battle of Sole Bay between the allied fleets of England and France under the Duke of York and the Dutch fleet under De Ruyter. The allied fleet was surprised by De Ruyter whilst at anchor. The French ships soon sheered off and the fighting was mainly between the English and the Dutch. It was a grim struggle. The Dutch Vice-Admiral Van Ghent was killed and De Ruyter was wounded. On the English side the Earl of Sandwich was blown up with his flagship the *Royal James* and five other ships were lost. An old ballad describes how

> They battered without let or stay
> Until the evening of that day,
> 'Twas then the Dutchmen ran away;
> The Duke had beat them tightly.

But no trustworthy historian confirms the ballad writer's account and it remains uncertain whether the victory was with the English or the Dutch.

3

THE SENSE
OF THE PAST

HISTORIC buildings such as castles and abbeys naturally stimulate thoughts of other ages. In Suffolk it is not only in such places that the past asserts itself more strongly than the present: in almost every small town and village the laws of time seem to have been mysteriously suspended. Remote influences are at work in the ancient streets; it is as if a spell has been laid upon them, which even at midday is unbroken. You may pass from end to end of these little towns and scarcely meet a soul. With your presence you will stir the deep silence. Perhaps you will ring a shop bell and summon the listless tradesman from his room at the back. But all your efforts will be no more than a faint puff of wind on a sultry summer day. The old houses lean towards each other as if seeking support after centuries of top-heaviness. The strange devices on the plastered façades and on the spandrels of the doorways are eloquent of bygone crafts and customs. The guildhall, unchanged since it was founded, and the great church speak of a vanished community and of an active, prosperous past. These towns and villages seem to have lost all inclination to advance hundreds of years ago. This is the source of their irresistible, tranquil charm.

Long Melford village street must be one of the longest in England. It continues for more than a mile flanked by a variety of houses and cottages, some timbered, some plastered and coloured pink, white and yellow, some, built by the coconut matting and horsehair weavers in the nineteenth century, of grey and red brick. One bears on its façade the name *Coconut House* in ginger-brown lettering, another tall thin house of grey brick displays an astonishing parapet of thickly ornamented tracery painted Naples yellow and a bow window supported by Moorish pillars. The street ends suddenly at the village green, a fair, wide expanse of luxuriant, flowery grass sloping up to a group of gigantic elms, to the almshouses built by Sir William Cordell and to the lengthy battlemented outline of the church. On the right the red brick walls and mitred turrets of Long Melford Hall emerge from a background of park and trees. A moat, dry and overgrown in summer, surrounds the house and it is further protected by a venerable wall which ends at the gateway in an octagonal summerhouse. Old stone steps bleached by the weather and stained by patches of dark green moss lead from the door of the summerhouse into the garden. And parallel to it on the green is an octagonal conduit which once supplied the moat with water. The house was recently damaged by fire, but its noble façade rises unchanged above the wall to confront the broad green and the row of low cottages far away on the opposite side. Some of them are gabled, some are unbelievably thin, others are fat, white and plastered, and before them all are long gardens full of old-fashioned flowers—forget-me-nots, stocks, daisies, wallflowers, canterbury bells and candytuft. It is a romantic scene, curiously hushed even on a sunny May morning. The voice of the cuckoo rings across the empty green, nothing stirs or sounds in the dusty street behind.

It is but three miles from Long Melford to Lavenham. The road is high, with changing views over the rolling landscape. This and the clear, fresh air give the momentary impression of a mountain top. Suddenly above the brow of a slight hill the immense grey tower of Lavenham church leans dramatically against the sky. Within a few moments the whole of this great building bursts upon the eye. The face of the tower is now seen to be packed with hundreds of thousands of dark shining flints and decorated with shields and with bands of roses and stars. From above the high, clear windows and the battlemented walls soars a pinnacle clustered with ornament and culminating in a delicately crowned weathervane. The pierced parapets, carved with wheat sheaves and with stars, are surmounted by seated figures, headless and grave. All the shields bear the arms of Thomas Spryng, a rich clothier of Lavenham, who bore the cost of the great building, married his daughter to Aubrey de Vere, son of the Earl of Oxford, and when he died in 1523 left £200 for the completion of Lavenham tower and orders that a thousand masses should be said for his soul.

Below the church, tumbling first downhill then climbing up to the market place are the cream and pink houses, the timbers and the red roofs of the sixteenth century. Nothing much but an inconspicuous row of Victorian almshouses and one or two cottages at the far end of the village near the station has been added for more than three hundred years. In the unreal, medieval streets—Water Street, Lady Street, Prentice Street, Church Street and Market Street—the eye is bewildered by the dazzling striped pattern made by the quantity of beams, by the great number of nodding gables and by the oddly carved heads peering from unlikely corners. The finest of all these ancient buildings is the former hall of the Guild of Corpus Christi, a timber-framed house with an oak door, tall stout chimneys and irregular gables. A figure carved on the corner post, holding a distaff and the charter of the Guild, represents John de Vere, the founder. This perfectly preserved Guildhall, the old Wool Hall in the next street, the silent market square where a touch of egg-shell blue on one of the houses heightens the red of the roofs and the pink plaster of its neighbours are seen as if in a trance. The unsubstantial dream-like impression is increased by the sight of a tabby cat sleeping in the empty window of a tailor's shop. Only the notice of a forthcoming sale posted outside Shilling Old Grange and dated 1947 breaks the illusion and carries a breath of reality into this bewitched place.

The awareness of the past, so vivid at Lavenham, can be experienced all over Suffolk. At Kersey, which is like a miniature Lavenham, at Monks Eleigh, at Chelsworth and Lindsey, at Monewden, deep in the heart of green lanes, at Earl Soham where a white windmill shines through the foliage of huge trees and nightingales sing in the garden of the stately Elizabethan rectory, the sense of another age predominates. Hartest is one of the most beautiful of these forgotten, enchanted villages. It lies at the foot of a steep hill remote from main roads. The church is not built on the height as is usual in Suffolk, but hidden away at one corner of the green in a valley by a stream. It is a wild, overgrown spot with all the appearance of either neglect or sorcery. A high, untrimmed holly hedge screens the churchyard, the path to the wide porch of square, dressed flints is thick with brambles, spreading yews block the windows, the tombstones struggle to free themselves from a blanket of ivy, stunted willows and burberry bushes grow amongst the graves. Yellow and red cottages fringe the far spreading green, among them a modest Congregational Church of unexpectedly exquisite proportions and design. Probably it was built by the Dutch refugees who came to this part of the country in the seventeenth century. It is of yellow plaster with a dark pantiled roof. On each side of the pointed and pilastered porch are long, slender arched windows. From the sharply inclined roof two tiny dormer windows echo the form of the entrance arch. To the right a small gabled wing has a narrow, brown, fanlighted door squeezed in at the side nearest to the main building and two arched windows one above the other. It is the most perfect of the many meeting houses of Dutch origin scattered about Suffolk. Another lovely example is the square red brick hall at Wrentham, dated 1663. With its shining brown tiles and double row of arched windows it is like one of those houses seen in the pictures of Pieter de Hooch.

The romantic aspect, the mellowed peace of Hartest are repeated on a larger scale at Clare. There is the same sense of arrested time here, although the little town is bright with fresh white paint and newly plastered walls. On a high mound above the streets are the ivy choked ruins of a Norman castle. The slopes of the mound are dense with undergrowth, twisting trees and prickly hawthorns so that it is impossible to find a way through them. They make a dark background to the shining little town with its wide, quiet streets and pleasant market square. Among the old-fashioned shops inscribed with the graceful

lettering of the eighteenth century is one with a high, curved Georgian window bearing over it the name STIFF in raised capitals of mottled blue and white enamel. It is a saddle-maker's shop full of bridles, ropes, straps and walking sticks and in the centre of the window stands a small, elegant white plaster horse. In a street opposite Stiff's the Half Moon and the Swan Inn stand side by side. A blue glass lantern with a white moon on it swings over the doorway of the first named, while on the front of the Swan there hangs an extraordinary carving of a swan wearing a crown round its neck and chained to a tree. Close by is the church where red brick mingles with flint rubble in the broad tower and crocketed turrets; and overlooking the churchyard is a pargeted house with the date 1473 which attracts more than ordinary attention. The brown roof is covered with lichen, the base of the bow window is carved with fat-stemmed flowers and two scaly devils holding a shield; and the large, bold, florid design of leaves, flowers and loops on the walls is one of the most striking examples of pargeting in a district where this form of decoration abounds. Like many of the patterns found on houses in West Suffolk it is more Renaissance than medieval in flavour. So it is interesting to discover that the families who in Tudor times were enriched by the woollen trade, employed French and Italian plasterers to ornament their homes. English plasterers were influenced by them and the flamboyant foreign style thus embellishes the walls of many a simple Suffolk cottage.

Many of these silent, sleeping towns and villages were once wealthy, animated industrial centres. The story told by Jocelyn of Brakelond and immortalised by Carlyle of the old women of Bury rushing out to brandish their distaffs in the faces of the monastic tax gatherers would suggest that cloth was made in Bury before the end of the twelfth century. Records show that weaving was carried on at that time all along the borders of Suffolk and Essex and that the trade was concentrated at Had-

Chelsworth

leigh, Hadleigh which with its long street of pale, plaster-fronted houses, its timbered guildhall and towered deanery now resembles nothing so much as a beautiful shell long since emptied of life and robbed of its colour. After the immigration of the Flemings in 1236 the woollen trade grew in importance and by the middle of the fourteenth century weaving had in many districts become the principal occupation of the people, not only in the larger towns of Ipswich, Bury, Stowmarket and Sudbury but in a great number of villages, some of which like Lavenham and Long Melford became as populous and prosperous as towns and built the magnificent churches whose size so amazes us today.

The state papers of Elizabeth's reign contain many references to the Suffolk industry. There we can trace the course of the wool from the back of the sheep through every process of manufacture and exchange until it is stored away as dyed cloth of many colours in the hold of an Ipswich trading vessel. As it crosses the sea it may fall a prey to pirate or enemy. But if it reaches its destination we can watch the merchants of Flanders or Spain bargaining over it, or perhaps see it pass immediately into the hands of some Levantine trader who will fashion it into garments for the Turk or the Muscovite.

The greater part of the wool was dyed blue, but violet, purple and green were also common. The chief materials used in dyeing the wool were woad and indigo, and there were three varieties of colours, blues, azures and plunkets. The carding and spinning were done by women and children in their cottage homes all over

Suffolk, and in institutions such as Christ's Hospital the children were set to card and spin from their earliest years. An order of 1570 states that every spinster was

to have 6 lb. of wool every week and to bring the same home every Saturday night, and if any fail so to do the clothier to advertise the constable thereof for the examination of the cause, and to punish it according to the quality of the fault.

The spinners, having no organisation of their own, were frequently oppressed and it is not surprising to find them sometimes keeping back part of the wool given out to them and making up the weight by the addition of moisture to the yarn. There was discontent, too, because many weavers were reduced to the position of poor servants while others became wealthy clothiers. Nevertheless the woollen trade of Suffolk prospered until the middle of the seventeenth century. Then internal friction, mismanagement and foreign competition gradually reduced the looms to idleness and the countryside to poverty. In 1642, when the clothiers had more than £35,000 of unsaleable broadcloth on their hands, they decided to appeal to Charles I. There is something of unspeakable pathos about the story of how these Suffolk men advanced towards the King and implored his aid as he descended from his carriage at Greenwich. He was too deeply preoccupied with his own misfortunes to give ear to the petitioners. The Stuart monarchy and the Suffolk cloth industry were both doomed and came to grief at almost the same moment.

By the beginning of the eighteenth century, weaving had come to a standstill all over the county, though wool was combed and spun for the weavers of other counties and there were a few curious survivals from the old Eastland trade such as the calimancoes woven at Lavenham as late as 1804 for export to Russia where the Tartars wore them as sashes. The accounts of eighteenth-century travellers in Suffolk are full of vivid descriptions of the roadside spinners, and in 1800 Arthur Young still cites the carding and spinning of wool as the chief occupation of the people. But by 1840 the trade was practically extinct, lingering on only in Sudbury until 1871.

In some of the old weaving centres other branches of the textile industry sprang up. At Long Melford and at Sudbury horsehair materials and coconut matting were made, and at Ipswich and Stowmarket sacking and sailcloth were woven from the hemp which grew plentifully on both the north and south borders of Suffolk. But these in time dwindled away, too, and now there are but one or two solitary handweavers left in the county, romantic survivors of the past. All the bustle of such places as Long Melford, Lavenham, Lindsey, Kersey and Hadleigh has been swallowed up in silence, leaving behind the guild halls where the clothiers bargained over their work, the churches they built, the houses where the spinners and weavers plied their trade and a strange sense of the active life that once informed them.

4

THE CHURCHES

Some of the characteristics of the Suffolk churches have already been mentioned, for it is not possible to describe any part of the county without some allusion to the great buildings which dominate the landscape. I have touched upon two romantic aspects, that they are frequently of vast size and that they are often found in lonely situations, deep in a grassy meadow or towering above some obscure little village of less than a dozen scattered cottages. The size of the structures has been accounted for by the story of Suffolk's bygone prosperity. The wealthy merchants and clothiers of the fourteenth and fifteenth centuries made their influence felt and expressed their charity by building and embellishing a great church. The size was not always dictated by the population but by motives of thankfulness and devotion, flavoured not seldom by ostentation, the desire to rival a neighbour's building.

There are many round-towered churches in Suffolk, towers of every size and shape of roundness, squat and thick, tall and thin, and most of them are to be found along the Waveney Valley. But it is the square-towered churches which received their final form when the woollen trade was at its height which distinguish the county. Externally they are of striking individuality. The beautiful surfaces of towers and walls are of flint, occasionally used in its natural state but more often knapped smooth. From about 1450 the flints were used for ornamental purposes and ingeniously patterned with the thin slabs of freestone in the manner known as flushwork. Elaborate decorations were applied to clerestory, porch and tower. Sometimes, as at Woolpit, the design is in stone with a filling of split flints, sometimes the flint forms a dark background for a tracery of freestone, as at Coddenham. The most usual devices are saints' emblems, shields and flowers, and the striking black and white shapes can be seen a great way off. Eye and Southwold are famed examples, but many wayside churches such as Glemsford, Stanstead and Gipping are equally richly patterned.

Of the impressive exteriors, the exciting, dramatic situations of the Suffolk churches it is not possible here to describe more than a few favourites. Lavenham has been portrayed, and the great length of Long Melford has already been glimpsed above the village green. At Fornham All Saints the tower dwarfs a few thatched houses, at Cavendish the church nestles among a group of ochre-washed cottages like an old hen with her brood. Dennington, crumbling and ivy-grown, with battlemented tower and canopied niches over windows and porch, leaves a memory of wild, desolate beauty. Stoke-by-Nayland, often painted by Constable, is a grand and solemn sight. It has a long nave with an embattled parapet, much old faded brick-work, and a majestic pinnacled tower that seems to soar over the surrounding countryside and lean towards the Stour. The position of Blythburgh is unsurpassed. It stands besides the river in the heart of a vast marshland, a great, silvery-grey mass among a few tumbledown cottages, the relics of a once prosperous port. It is the loneliest church in Suffolk; its exquisite proportions and delicate tracery are perfectly outlined against the sky from every side for miles around, strangely contrasted with the flat, encompassing wilderness of fen, heath and stream. After a long period of decay Blythburgh has been repaired and cared for. The aisle parapets are particularly fine; they have pinnacles surmounted by figures, two of which represent Christ and the Virgin, while the others are demoniac and symbolic of vices. Under the east window is a series of crowned letters which have never yet been interpreted.

The interiors of the Suffolk churches, varying from the sumptuousness of Lavenham or Mildenhall to the simple white-washed nave and swinging oil lamps of Stanstead, offer an abundance of delights. The interior of Long Melford, though less elaborate than Lavenham, is among the most inspiring of the larger churches. The first impression is of light and space. The walls seem to be composed nearly all of glass through which nothing can be seen but an expanse of sky. There is no mysterious gloom; the atmosphere is as translucent as the crystal water of a mountain lake where not a single pebble is blurred. The association with water is encouraged by the odd, tiny panes of light green glass which here and there interrupt the colourless window space. Only three windows are filled with old stained glass, the east and the two west of the aisle, and even here the predominating pale yellow colour suggests water. Among the figures which occupy the large lights of these windows are thirty-one remarkable portraits all showing interesting details of dress; they include Sir William Howard, Richard Pygot and Sir Thomas Montgomerie, Elizabeth, Countess of Oxford, Elizabeth Talbot and Elizabeth Tilney.

DIEV ET MON DROIT.

PART

PETER REALL.

IPSWICHE

A	Chrifts church	G	S.Laurence	N	S.Mary Key
B	S.Georgs chap.	H	S.Stephens	O	Stoke church
C	S.Margarets	I	S.Albons	P	Stoke Br bridge
D	S.Mathews	K	S.Clements	Q	Stoke mill
E	S.Mary Tower	L	S.Nicolas	S	The Key
F	S.Mary Elms	M	S.Peters.	T	Graye Friers

The Salt Water

Orwell flu

The Dvkes, and Earles of Clare, created fince the Normans conquest

Gilbert de Clare Earle of Clare.

Lionell fonn to K E 3 Duke of Clarence

Thomas Lancastre Duke of Clarence

Georg: Brother to K E 4 Duke of Clarence

NORFOLKE

& Downham

Wilton

Hockhold

Wetinge

Litle Ouse Flu.

Downeham

Wangforde

Brandon

Thetforde

Rushworth Ridlesworth Gasthe

Firret Ouse flu

Lakenheathe

Eldn

Knattefhall

Weston

The

LACKFORD HVN

Bernham

E. Euston

Crowveston Hepton

Efenell

Fakenham pua

Fakenham mag

Fakenham pua

BLACK BORN

Mildnall

Wordwell

Hynnyton

Beringham

R

Jfelham

W: Stow

Leuermere pua

Troston

Sapfton Hepworth

Stanton

Fordham

Worlington

Frecknham

Ixlinham

Berton

Lack forde

Flempton

Leuermere mag

Culforth

Ingham

Ixworthe e thorpe.

Bardwell

Langham the

Herningfwell

Tuddenham

Hengraue

Rifhye

Fernham genefeit

Timpton

Fernham omnium Sanctorum

Ixworthe

Pakenham

Hunston

Stowlangtoft

Badwell

Norton

Afhfelde

Baddingham Kennet

Cam:ham

THINGOW HVN

THEDWARDSTRE

HVN

Exninge

Kenforde

Gaiefley

Saxham magna

Wfley

Saxhm pua

Rougham

Fernham martin Berton

Burye

Dreben

Thurfton

Tostok

Elmeswell

Wi

Newmerket

Moulton

Denham

Barrowe

Cheuington

Herninghe the

Ikfworth

Newton

Rufhbrok

Whelnetham pua

Munkebradfeld

Heffet

S. Cleres bradfeld

Drenkeston

Ratlesden

Shelland

Ockь

CAM:

Afhley

Dalham

Ouefden

Hauefted

Weltham magna

Gedding

Buxhall

Findon

BRIDGE

Cheuely

Cathrige

Lidgate

Chedber

Whepsted

Rede

Burnebradsfeld

Felfham

Cock, feld

Brettenham Wattefham

a

Carleton

Cowilder

Wrckham brooke

Debden

Brokley

Langfhill

Thorpe

COSFORD

Weston

Bradley mag

Thirlow pua

Bradley pua

Druston

Haukden

Somerten

Kettlebaston

HV Buston

Hitcham

Bilston stre

SHIRE

Wickham

Carleton

Stradishill

Bernardston

Stanfelde

Hartyste

Shimplinge

Prefton

Munke Illeigh

Nat

Wickham

Horsheath

Tallow twratting

Wratting pua

Wirhersfeilde Hauerill

Honedon

Boxted

Alpheton

Burntey

Laneham

Lynsey

Chefl

Shedi campes

Kediton

Poslingforde

ERISBRYGE

Glemysforde

Stansfed

BABER

Mellinge

Castle scampes

Sturmere

HVN

Wickhо

Clare

Stoke

Candishe

Acton

Melforde

HVN

Waldingfeilde pua

Groton

Edwardston

Burbrok

Afhden

Egherels

Chilton

Waldingfeild mag

Newton

Boxford

Ouington

Poules heltham

Lyston

Nedging

Afmonton

Peotlowe

Boreley

Bullington

Sudburye

Cornerd pua

Cornerd magi

Smakebridge

Buers

Stoke

Brunden

Mulleton

Henny

Lammersh

Buers hamlet

Nevi

Weston

PART OF

PART OF

Warningford

Hersley

| 1 | 2 | 3 | 4 | 5 | 6 | 7 | 8 | 9 | 10 |

THE SCALE OF ENGLIS MILES

Cum Privilegu

SUFFOLKE described
and divided into Hundreds, The situa:
tion of the fayre towne IPSWICH shewed,
with the ARMES of the most noble fami:
lies that have bene either Dukes, or Earles
both of that Countie as also of Clare.

A SCALE OF PASES

V Black Friers   4 Barre Gatt
W Chrift Hospitall   5 Old Bar gate
X Gramer Schole   6 Fishe market
Y Poores houses   7 Kings Strete
Z Hasford mull   8 Cornt hill
1 Bull Gatt   9 Broke Street

BOADICIA

THE DUKES and
EARLES of SUFFOLK
Created since the Normás
conquest

Robert Vfford. Erle
of Suffolk

William de la poole
Duke of Suffolk.

Charles brandon duke
of Suffolk.

Henry Gray duke
of Suffolk.

Thomas Howard Earle
of Suffolke.

Yarmouth
Vermouthauē
Burgh Bradwell
east Delton Gorleston
Frifton Hopton
Alhby
St Olaves Lounde
Hormnflet HVN.Corton
Somerley Blunston
Wheataker townc
Flixton Leitoft
Alby Oldton
Kirtlow
Gillingham Mutford bridge
Kelfton Carleton
Wrentham Barnhyz
Eftingham Barsham Beckles MVTFORD
Dichingham Iugate Mutforde Gislan
Erifham Shepemeaowe Meiringham Weston N.Couc HVN Keslande
Ringesfield Ellowe Kufbmere
Bungay St Andrs Henfted
Flixton Southelman St Johns Shanfeld Sterley Benaker
Rednall St Mergret WANGFORD HV Redsham Wrentham
Harlefton St Peters St Michael Steuen S Coue Couc
Nedeham Homerfeld St Laurent Brampton Vageshall S Crenton hith
Brodife S Margaret Croft Spekfall Easton
Thorp St Nicolas Alsanct Rumboro Wetfall Sotheron Barkers
Billingford Wastoft Wangford
Dis Sylam Wetherfdall S James Linsfed Whifet Holton Bliford Roydon
Osmondfton Hoxon Fresenfeld Chefton Halesworth Saxouildc
HOXON HV Metfeld Linsted mag Cokeley Wenhafton Dunwiche
Horham Huntafeld Bramsfeld
Stradbrok Laxfeld Vppcton Walpole Thorington Walderswicd
Denham Heueningham Sibton BLITHING HV
Wilbye Brunsffe Baddingham Darfhm Mifmere
Redlinsfeld Dunnyngton Peasfall Yoxford hauen
Illington Southolt Waringsworth Kelfall Fordley Wetfelton
Bedingsfeld Bedfeld Tawyfton Cransford Brusyard Midleton Theberton
Muckfwam Soxted Sweflinge Renah Carlton
Framingham Glemhm ma Stratford Saxmundhm Aldringham
Kelteborough Benhall Sternfeld
Kenton Afhfeld Glemham par Knathall Laytson
LOES Thorp Brandefta Easton Farnhm Sifwell
Debenham Crettingham Hachefton Marlesforde Snape Thorp
Wickhm Blaxall Frifti Aldringham
Meneden Hoo Afh PLOMES Dunnyngsworth Hafilwood
TREDLINGE Penftric GATE HV Iken Sudburne Aldebrough
Petaugh Dalinghoo Rendlesham Chillesforde
HVN: Framflem Charfefeld Vfforde Eyke Orforde
Otley Clopton Melton Butley
Hemingham Debache Hecketon Brumfwall Orford hauen
Cretingh Afhbocking Boufler Bealing ma Sutton Bovton
Nedcham Swetland Culpho Shatfham WILFORDE
Grundsboro Bealing par Woodbridge Holley HVN
MERE Hench Burgk Playford Neettleham Rammefholt
Cobham Barhm Akenham Kefgrant Bright.well Waldringafelde Alderton
Dermuden Blakkfm ma Cleydt Rushmere Hemley
Netlefted Weftersfeld CARLEFORD Newborne Bawdfley
CLEYDON Whitton Brighr.well HV
Blakenhm fug mont IPSWICHE Buckleham
HVN Bramford Foxall Kirton
Bussfall Nacton COLNES
Washbrok Sproughton Stoke HVN Felkenham
Copdock Freston Lennington Felixtow
Bentley Belfted gua Wherfted Trimleis
Tatingeston Woluerfton Chempton HVN:
Wenham pua Helbrok SAMFORDE Walton
herbolt Brantham Sutton Harkfeld Langerffon
Catwade bridee Shetley Orwel hauen
Lauford Miftley Arwerton
am Manitre Harwiche
Bradfeld
Ramfey
Dower courts

ESSEX

Performed by Iohn Speede and are to be solde in
Popes-head alley against the Exchang by George Hūble

Just outside the screen on the wall of the north aisle is an alabaster relief of the kind which became popular during the fourteenth century, a long, wide panel representing the Adoration of the Magi. The figures are smoothly and simply treated. The Virgin reclines while the elderly-looking child stands upright in her lap; the foremost of the wise men raises one hand to his headdress as if to remove it; two oxen peep from under the bed. There are traces of red and blue colouring on the relief and the whole is surrounded by a neatly finished edge as if the composition were like a painting, intended for individual exhibition. In both the North and South Chapels there are some attractive brasses. A knight, whose legs are much too large for his body, lies with his head on his helmet. He has huge moustaches, a great chin and humorous eyes. A lady nearby looks to the left, clasps her hands and wears an ornate, conical headdress. Her long neck is bare, a rich cloak covers a boldly patterned gown. Both are members of the Clopton family of Kentwell Hall who were the principal builders of the church. Just beyond the brasses is the Clopton Chantry where elaborately carved scrolls interlaced with foliage and flowers form a continuous painted ornament round the cornice of the roof. The colours, fast fading, are green, red and gold and on the scrolls are verses by John Lydgate, the Monk of Bury.

John Clopton of Kentwell built the Lady Chapel at Long Melford, which adjoins the church, though it must be separately entered. It is as large as many a parish church. The whole is a rectangle with an inner chapel surrounded on all sides by what its founder called a cloister. The roof above this embracing aisle is wonderfully carved with leaves, scrolls, clasping hands, sunflowers, oaksprays, thistles and roses. The beams are supported by angels bearing urns, torches, censers and shields. With their wild, backward flying hair and outstretched wings they appear just to have alighted on their perches.

Great angels with outstretched wings are a feature of the famous hammerbeam roofs of East Anglia. The fluttering wings of the angel host sometimes spread all over the roof, catching the imagination, though the figures are often rough and clumsy when they are detached from their positions. Two of the most splendid angel roofs in Suffolk are at Mildenhall and at the little village of Grundisburgh. At Grundisburgh there are three tiers of angels spread over the double hammerbeam structure of the roof. At Mildenhall the hammer beams rest upon fantastic stone heads, grimacing, frowning, protruding their tongues, and between each of them gigantic angels shelter saints beneath their wings. In the spandrels extraordinary scenes and figures disclose themselves: a fierce woman in a horned headdress, a roguish pig wearing a collar, two monkeys, one playing an organ, the other blowing bellows, and a demon catching a dog by his tail, mingle with biblical figures. The roof of the nave itself is covered by a host of angels, two very large and more than fifty lesser ones, some holding books and others playing upon stringed instruments.

Woodcarving, especially of bench ends and misericordes, reaches the highest perfection in East Anglia. There are fine examples all over Suffolk, illustrating every aspect of medieval life and thought. At Blythburgh the stall fronts are carved with figures in relief of the apostles, Stephen, John Baptist, Christ and the Virgin. As is traditional in Suffolk, Philip has three loaves and Jude a boat. Some of the remarkable bench-end figures illustrate the occupations of the months, reaping, the vintage, sowing, killing a pig, warming the feet, holding a flower, tying up faggots, the Works of Mercy (a man in bed), a man sitting in the stocks with his hands chained down and a collar on his neck, and the Seven Deadly Sins. At Fressingfield the fronts and backs of the seats are patterned. One specially noteworthy is known as the Passion Bench and is decorated with a series of shields bearing the emblems of the Passion, the cock, the buffeting hand and a jug; the pillar, scourges and cords; the cross, the crown of thorns and nails; the reed and the sponge, and the lance in saltire; the ladders, pincers and hammers; the seamless robe and three dice on a board. Next to this is another bench with devices appropriate to SS. Peter and Paul. The benches at Great Bealings are covered with an astonishing variety of carving. A swan sits on her nest among bulrushes; there are a rhinoceros, a long-haired dog, a starfish on a scallop shell and a fine Negro's head. A little old lady perches on the edge of a chair, a mailed fist clasps a dagger, a hand clutches an oak branch, a smiling woman holds two fish and the wild man whom we meet everywhere in Suffolk brandishes his bludgeon. Another strange figure frequently found among the Suffolk carvings is that known as Sciapus. There is one on a bench end at Dennington. He lies on his back and holds his huge foot over himself to shield him from the sun. Such creatures, according to the medieval belief, were the inhabitants of South Africa.

At Acton the carvings on the poppy heads are more worthy of attention than the brass of Sir Robert de Bures for which the church is famous. The poppy heads have been enriched with every local variety of wild flower, leaf and bird, all recognisable although conforming to a pattern. Two young pheasants peck wheat amongst which corncockles are growing, a thrush enjoys a bunch of grapes, a wood-pigeon perches with an oakleaf in his mouth, and on one of the pews the artist has carved his name, C. Newson. Among the misericordes at Lavenham a great pelican, carved almost in the round, tears at its breast to nourish two tiny birds in a nest below. A male and female devil are making diabolical music. One, with cloven feet and a long tail, smiles hideously as he plays with crutches upon a bellows. His companion clasps a viol while from below her skirt a dragon tail swings out to the right between her scaly legs. The so called Spryng pew or parclose in the south aisle at Lavenham is one of the most

skilful and elaborate carvings in England. Of incredible elegance and delicacy it is Renaissance rather than medieval in feeling. In the arches are cunning designs of tracery composed of foliage, flowers, shields and writhing creatures. Winged lions, dragons, jesters with tails, men climbing trees and animals chasing terrified children fill the ornamental panels below, and in the niches of the festooned corner posts are the figures of St. Catherine with her wheel and St. Blaise, patron of weavers, holding the comb with which his murderers combed the flesh from off his body.

In the fifteenth century, when East Anglia was the scene of so much church building, figure decoration was again used on fonts which for two hundred years had been simply ornamented with mouldings or a band of foliage. It is therefore not surprising that important developments in this direction are to be found in Suffolk. Typical examples are the fonts at Westhall and at Orford. At Westhall the font is carved with the baptism of Christ, the Seven Sacraments and a scene with a man doing penance. The base of the font at Orford is supported by clumsy lions alternating with Suffolk wild men or Wodehouses. The bowl rests on the demi-figures of angels with outspread wings and is divided by buttresses into oblong panels containing the Evangelist symbols and sacred figures such as the Trinity.

East Anglia was one of the foremost centres of painting in the middle ages and a great deal of work remains in the Suffolk churches. In the earlier panels such as the retable of Thornham Parva, of 1320, the style is closely allied to that of manuscript painting. The retable consists of nine upright arched panels painted in tempera. The spandrels between the arches are filled with shallow carvings of enormous English wild roses, buds and foliage. The central panel represents the Crucifixion, and saints are ranged on either side, the slender, elongated figures appearing against a background of patterned gold. A linear rhythm unites all the panels, the figures glance towards each other with eloquent gestures and they are further bound together by the colour design of purple-pink, white, brown, yellow-green and red. In the Crucifixion scene the figure of Christ is turned slightly towards the Virgin, who inclines her head tenderly, clasping her long hands in anguish, while St. John stands sorrowfully apart. It is an intensely poetical and poignant composition.

Fifteenth-century screens in Suffolk are frequently painted. At Southwold the rood and aisle screens are decorated with the figures of prophets, angels and saints emerging from a background of white and gold, framed by deep, ornate moulding and surmounted by tendril-like clusters of tracery. In an attempt to give recession to the pictures, the personages are each placed on a tiled platform, but the general impression is of rich, flat pattern. The figures lack form and animation. Many of the heads are scarred and damaged and those of the apostles, repainted by Richmond, have acquired a Tennysonian air of solemnity quite out of keeping with the rest of the panels. At Somerleyton there are figures of much greater liveliness and individuality. They appear against a background of unrelieved red or green; the haloes make an unusual array of plain red, purple and green; the foregrounds are of brown earth or acid green grass. Interest is thus concentrated on the figures alone. These are short, with overlarge heads and prominent eyes. Formalism in the treatment of details such as the hair and the folds of the garments is combined with vigorous movement and subtle characterisation, while an easy rhythm of attitude connects the panels one with another. St. Laurence, dressed in purple, white and gold and clasping his gridiron in his right hand, appears to be walking towards the right, while with a turn of the head he looks back, a strange smile on his lips. The female saint on his left also smiles as she casts a sidelong glance towards her neighbour, King Edmund. St. Dorothy, crowned with flowers, is a plain type still common in East Anglia.

Most of the wall paintings in Suffolk, as elsewhere, have been obliterated. Among those which have survived, two subjects are conspicuous: St. Christopher and the Child, and the Doom. At Alpheton a St. Christopher, vast in size, faint and ill preserved, can just be made out on the nave wall facing the entrance. He has a plump bearded face and wears a little round straw hat. The celebrated Doom, at Wenhaston, is painted on rough boards. It was lost for centuries and was discovered in a curious manner. With other timber it had been removed to the churchyard where a heavy storm beat down upon it and removed the whitewash which had hidden it since the Reformation. The painting is believed to be the work of a Blythburgh monk. The Almighty sits on a rainbow with the Virgin and St. John the Baptist beside him, while below the Archangel Michael balances souls in the scale. The souls are nude, but they wear the headdresses of their trades or professions in earthly life. Peter welcomes the righteous at the doorway of Paradise and demons hustle the lost into eternal fire. The background is a beautiful dull green and the faces, like those at Somerleyton, are distinctly East Anglian.

Not only the fittings and features of the churches, but the Suffolk churchyards, flowery and overgrown, yield a variety of pleasures. Seventeenth-century tombstones with their bold designs of trumpeting angels, skulls, crowns, scrolls and garlands are common almost everywhere. There is a fine group of them at Lavenham. The inscription on Andrew Brown's headstone, of 1698, is enclosed in a thick oval of laurels above which grinning skulls and angels with outspread wings burst forth from clusters of leaves and flowers. Lichen growing on the eyeballs of one of the angels gives the face a disturbing, living expression. On another tomb two enormous skulls are divided by a pattern of hairbells and the raised tablet on which the florid

Opposite. Yachting near Orfo

inscription is written is bordered by the blossoms and spiky leaves of the hairbell. At Stanstead and Hartest there are some unusual gravestones, dating from the first half of the nineteenth century. The villages are near neighbours and the stones are probably all the work of the same man. The decorations are not the customary formal patterns, but compositions in relief. Over the names of William Watkinson and his wife Elizabeth, at Stanstead, is carved a realistic representation of Stanstead church and churchyard enlivened by the figure of an angel flying through the sky at break-neck speed, holding a floating scroll and blowing a long trumpet. At Hartest a gravestone of 1803, shows the sacrifice of Isaac. Abraham, a commanding figure, occupies the centre of the relief. He looks up astonished at an angel who appears with upraised arm from a rolling cloud while with his left hand he holds the nude victim in position on the pyre which is already kindled. To the right a tree springs from a great rock; on the left a poetical figure sits at the foot of a rock and another leads an ass towards him. It is a swirling, vigorous, imaginative conception executed with an intensity of feeling for which one might seek in vain in the religious paintings of the time.

There are epitaphs to suit all tastes. My own favourite is at Bramfield on the tombstone of Bridget Applethwaite, who died in 1773. It runs:

After the fatigue of a married life, borne by her with incredible patience, and after the enjoyment of the glorious freedom of an early and unblemished widowhood, she resolved to run the risk of a second marriage, but death forbade the banns.

5

THE HOME OF THE FLINT KNAPPERS

THE flint which plays so important a part in the composition of the Suffolk churches comes from one of the wildest tracks of country in England, the stretch of heath, warren and fir wood in the north-west corner of the county known as Breckland. Between Bury and Brandon the aspect of the landscape undergoes a surprising change. Coarse bracken and barren marshland take the place of ploughed fields and green meadows. There are no more cows, no more black-faced Suffolk sheep. The friendly oak and elm are supplanted by spinneys of stunted birch trees and by dense belts of firs planted by the Forestry Commission. The road is bordered by pines, twisted by the winds into grotesque shapes, not one grown to its full height. It is a scene of desolation resembling the chaos of the primeval universe described by Ovid. For many miles there is no sign of human habitation; herons fish undisturbed by reedy pools, the high-pitched cry of the stone curlew, the harsh call of the pheasant echo through the wastes. Rare flowers grow there, some of them survivors of the time when an arm of the sea reached this territory, the Golden Dock, Centaury, Sand Sedge, Yellow Vetch and the Spanish Catchfly. The few villages lie remote from each other, lost in the pine forests. Wangford is little more than a church; Eriswell consists of but a few cottages and its old manor house.

Unsavoury, sinister tales are told about the Breckland heath. It is said to have been the scene of the crime which originated the legend of the Babes in the Wood. Elveden is associated with the memory of a gamekeeper called Mar who was done to death by poachers. Another gamekeeper was killed in the vicinity many years ago and his body deposited in a chalk pit. With his latest breath he swore to haunt his murderers and still at dead of night a hearse, coffin and bearers may be seen to emerge from the pit. A tree near Euston is reputed to have sprung from a stake with which the body of a pirate, Chunk Harvey, was pierced when he was executed on this spot. A spectre known as the White Rabbit is thought to haunt Thetford Warren. It rushes by with enormous flaming eyes portending disaster. The headless ghost of the Archdeacon of Sudbury walks near the site of his murder on Temple Bridge, Icklingham.

The only sizeable place in Breckland is Brandon. It lies on the Norfolk border, a straggling little town of flint-walled, red-roofed houses on either bank of the Little Ouse. A five-arched bridge of medieval irregularity crosses the river, the natural stronghold of idlers and a coign of vantage from which to watch the swifts swooping and crying about the housetops, and to follow the course of the slow stream through a landscape of sandhills and marsh where starveling alders and melancholy pines stand knee-deep in water. Brandon boasts a flourishing trade in the preparation of rabbit skins; tobacco is also grown there. But its chief glory, though it may soon become no more than a memory, is still its flint knapping.

The sounds of tapping which can sometimes be heard in the streets of Brandon have echoed through that place unaltered for centuries. Flint knapping is the most ancient trade in England and it is known nowhere but at Brandon. Flint weapons were made there by men of the Stone Age and the pits where they quarried the stone can still be seen over the Norfolk border at Grimes Graves. In one of them a fossilised antler was discovered which had been used as a pick axe over five thousand years ago.

When the trade was at its height the flint, which was used for tinders, gunflints, the building of houses and the ornamentation of churches, came from Lingheath Common. The ground there, bright with broom and with all chalk-loving plants, is honeycombed with pits. The stones lie in well marked strata or 'sases', of which the lowest is the most highly prized. The shaft is carried downwards by successive stages, placed at right angles to each other in a slanting direction, 'on the sosh' according to the local phrase. Through the solid walls burrows are then driven, radiating in a series of lyre-shaped patterns from the central opening. The digger works in a constrained posture, by the light of an electric lamp. He uses a one-sided iron pick with which he removes the chalk from the slab of flint and then prizes out the stone by the aid of a small crowbar. It is carried to the surface upon the head of a second workman and there it is stacked endways in heaps and covered with dried fern and fir boughs to prevent the sun and the wind from changing its colour. Each heap makes one cartload, known in the district as a 'jag'. No mechanical devices are used in the quarrying and there have never been more than a very small number of men, perhaps fifty, engaged in the work.

Breckland

The fashioning of the flint involves three stages, quartering, flaking and knapping. With a leather pad tied to his knee the workman first takes a blunt hammer and breaks up the rough stone into more convenient pieces, each about six inches square. The surfaces of the quartered flint are as smooth and black as polished ebony. Next the knapper uses a pointed hammer and proceeds to 'flake' the flint, a most delicate and difficult operation. In a few moments with strokes too sure and too fast for the eye to follow, he reduces the entire flint to scores of chips and a small conical core which is put aside for building purposes. The best flakes are from four to five inches in length and either four or three sided.

Holding one of these flakes with its face uppermost upon a stake of iron driven into a large oak block, the knapper trims it into shape with a flat hammer of peculiar construction. His movements are again so nicely calculated, so regular and so rapid as to be almost imperceptible. In less than six minutes the piece of untried stone is changed by the craftsman into a heap of gunflints in four different sizes—musket, carbine, horse and single pistol.

I have spoken of the quarrying of the flints because that seems to me to be an essential part of the knapper's trade. But only one local quarrier is now at work on Lingheath and he has no successor. The knappers are in a sorry plight. Matches have ousted tinders; synthetic flints are made in factories; nobody has built a flint cottage for generations; ornamental work for churches is rarely in demand. The trade survives in a manner which can only be described as ironic. The Brandon knappers make gunflints for barter with the natives of the Congo and North and Central Africa. When the uncertain demand of the negroes ceases, this prehistoric industry will have completed the cycle of its existence. There is no one to follow the present knappers. Their sons wish to know nothing of the venerable trade. They think they have something better to do than to pass all their lives on the lonely warren and learn an obsolete trade which would bring in no more than five shillings for a thousand flints.

6

THE RIVERS

AMONG the rivers of Suffolk, despite the association of the Stour with Constable, there is none so famed as the Wye, the Avon or the Severn, yet in no other part of England is the character of the landscape so much determined by the watery element. There are no sizeable rivers in Suffolk and few are navigable far inland, but the whole county is criss-crossed by a network of streams, most of them making their way towards the sea, though the Lark flows eastwards to join the Ouse in Cambridgeshire. The very boundaries of Suffolk are formed by rivers; the Waveney and the Little Ouse separate the county from Norfolk, the Stour divides Suffolk and Essex. And the course of all these waterways and of their many tributaries, even the least pretentious of them, tiny rills that run dry in summer, is marked by astonishing luxuriance, unimaginable verdure.

River scenes play a large part in memories of Suffolk. The anglers of Barton Mills on the Lark come first to mind, blissfully occupied by the dark mill pool. Fast flowing streams, some of them nameless, run down from the high land about Lawshall and their steep banks are the source of unforgettable experiences. At one point a square church tower inclines at an impossible angle above the green ridge, at another three brilliant kingfishers chase their reflections in the shingly brook. At Benton End, Hadleigh, the Brett so enhances the pastoral beauty of the scene that it becomes in recollection a significant image of all the fullness and peace of high summer. For so small a stream the water is here surprisingly wide. A pink house surrounded by yews stands against a golden-brown, corn-covered slope. Intensely green, flat meadows separate the house from the smooth river. Sheep graze on the opposite bank and blue-green dragonflies, coloured airborne sticks, jerk through the sharp light and shade of the August day.

More than half of the Suffolk villages lie on the banks of a river or stream. Sometimes, as at Kersey, a brook runs straight across the main street; often, as in the neighbourhood of Brent Eleigh and Lindsey, a whole district seems to be intersected by dozens of rivulets. Cottages peep from bowers of willow and alder or appear actually to stand in the stream, gardens are fringed by reeds, the quiet sounds and soft splashes of river creatures are continually heard. Each riverside village boasts its own type of bridge and many of them are

On the Stour near Bures

characterised by old stone quays and irregular red brick houses rising abruptly from the water.

River landscapes in Suffolk are immensely varied. Towards the coast, wide estuary views are common, not the headland prospects of the west and north of England of distant quicksilver coils, but long, slanting vistas from the summit of slopes which only seem considerable because the surrounding countryside is generally low-lying. I have already mentioned the marshy stretch seen from the hilly site of Burgh Castle. There the Waveney goes out into Breydon Water through a wide landscape of dykes and mills; the water recedes into the haze of the distant sea and loses itself in light. The spiralling shape of the Alde as it makes its tortuous way to the sea dominates the scene commanded by the gentle eminence of Iken. Seen from the churchyard wall the vast expanse of river serpentines through banks of oak-fringed bracken, over bleak marshland and past the flat, dark shape of a dense pinewood towards the sea. At high tide the silvery water touches the roots of the trees, then it falls away until nothing remains of it but a thin stream trickling through an ocean of gleaming mud. River birds of every kind come to feed on the exposed flats, curlew, redshank, shelduck and mallard. The raucous cries, the quacking, screaming and wailing of the birds and the stinging lash of the east wind blustering across the marsh, moaning among the tombstones and tearing at the reed thatch of Iken church, enter into every remembrance of the tidal reaches of the Alde. The comparatively narrow estuary of the Deben with its fishtail fork presents an altogether different picture. The more intimate beauty of this landscape best reveals itself in cloudless summer weather when white and madder sails move lazily by the meadow spits, by low-lying woods and past the stone quay of Waldringfield drowsing in afternoon heat.

The diverse character of the rivers is still more apparent inland. The Stour winds through water meadows and through rich, rolling folded lands where the grain rustles shoulder high. It is a river of locks and mills and of wooden bridges that take the footfall softly with no metallic coldness. Well-stocked gardens step back from the water, thatched and plastered cottages lie close to the banks ensnared in reeds and overgrown with willows. Those who imagine Suffolk to be a flat county should follow the course of the Stour. The slopes of its valley are steep and irregular with a truly dramatic moment at Stoke-by-Nayland where the church crowns an abrupt rise from the water. The Orwell, which above Ipswich mysteriously changes its name to Gipping, flows through a pastoral, park-like landscape until it reaches the compact little town of Stow-market. There it runs among the ancient buildings, giving a Flemish air to the place, especially near the railway station where it passes by a red brick turreted malthouse. The Deben behind Woodbridge is a shallow, frequently dry stream with shelving banks, a quiet green trench in the country-side, often thick with yellow irises and kingcups. The Alde breaks up near Little Glemham into a maze of tiny rivulets interlacing through an isolated territory of unkempt hedges, dense thickets, irregular meadows and tangled valleys. The villages in these parts, Saxtead, Parham, Great Glemham, Sweffling, are small and shel-tered, still basking in the atmosphere of a time remote from this when there was neither fret nor hurry. The inhabitants seldom venture far afield. Once, on asking my way of an old man I was told that the path which attracted me, a twisting, thick-leaved track, ran for a distance of three paddocks but that he had never had occasion to go farther in that direction.

The Little Ouse runs partly through Breckland and shares the strange character of this wild heath. The river courses through fens bordered by heathland, the former home of the great bustard and the silver-grey rabbit. Between the river and the marshy meadows is the haling path which has been built up to a higher level than the surrounding country. From some points along this path looking on a clear day, towards Cambridgeshire, the great western tower and lantern of Ely can be seen shining through the haze on the far off horizon. Navigation on the Little Ouse is made possible by peculiar constructions known as stanches serving the same pur-pose as locks. There are only thirty-two stanches in all England and twenty-six of these are in the fenland. The stanch stays the water by means of an oak door attached by chains to an axle at the end of which is an enormous wheel. In order to raise the door the operator treads the spokes of the wheel, thus winding up the chain, and then makes the door fast by an iron hook attached to the wheel. Beside the stanch door are one or sometimes two sluices or 'cloughs' as they are called locally, which help to regulate the height of the water, and beyond them is an overfall. Below the stanch there lies a clear pool, the 'stanch hole', a favourite place for fishing and bathing. The stanch at Santon Downham is one of the most beautiful riverside spots in the county. The gaunt frame of the stanch with its gigantic wheel imposes itself on the flat landscape and makes a patterned reflection in the full, placid river. The axle and its supports enclose a charming vista sweeping away to the tiny church of Santon, farmhouses and a glimpse of the moated remains of Santon House. Water avens grow not far from the haling path and both banks of the river are clothed with rank vegetation. The brilliant pink flower of the willow-herb makes with the purple spikes of the loose-strife a patch of oriental colour, the blue

Mill on the River Deben Estuary at Woodbridge

skullcap shines among creamy waves of meadow-rue and tall umbels of hemlock, the yellow of the fleabane and bur marigold is intensified by its proximity to the lilac-pink of the valerian. At the sound of a footstep on the path startled moorhens dash out from the undergrowth, a pair of noisy gadwall fly up and a little vole plops into the stream. Herons, coots and snipe are frequently seen and the kestrel hovers over the adjacent warren where the heather, known here by its old Scandinavian name of ling, grows to a height of three feet.

In its long sinuous course the Waveney would seem to embrace all the qualities of the other Suffolk rivers. Its source is close to that of the Little Ouse in the landscape peculiar to Breckland, it runs through meadows and cornfields as rich as those watered by the Stour, it receives as many tributaries as the Alde, it flows like the Gipping past the well-groomed parks of country seats, and it is sometimes secret and narrow like the upper reaches of the Deben so that small river craft seem suddenly to float mysteriously among buttercups, marsh-marigolds and cuckoo flowers. Yet the Waveney is entirely unlike any other river, it is at the same time more unobtrusive, more romantic, more desolate than any waterway in Suffolk. An atmosphere of great antiquity pervades it, perhaps because it is connected with so much of Suffolk's history, for Burgh Castle, Hoxne and Bungay all lie on the Waveney. The river flows, too, past other storied ruins and castles and by fantastic Elizabethan mansions. The broken walls and great gateway of Mettingham Castle crumble by the banks of the Waveney; Wingfield Castle built in the fourteenth century by Michael de la Pole, Earl of Suffolk, can be seen from the river; and the Tudor chimneys of Roos Hall rise from a forest of grey-green willows close to the water. The ancient walls of the garden go down into the very river. Gillyflowers, valerian, delicate ferns and stonecrop spring from crevices in the brickwork and below the level of the dark, secret water a tangled jungle of weeds sways with the current. The brown heads of bulrushes crowd on the opposite bank and from among them colonies of warblers watch the intruder. Otters are sometimes seen here, and near this spot an unusual form of fishing is carried on, known as eel-babbing. It is a complicated method of catching eels, only practised at night and only in those parts of the river where the bed is of gravel. The bait is made of worms and dung and threaded with wool instead of a hook. Only those who have made an eel-bab and caught an eel can say why wool should be better than a plain hook.

The upper reaches of the Waveney pass through country which is perhaps better described as untamed rather than desolate. Narrow winding lanes are found all over Suffolk, but nowhere are they so aimless, so labyrinthine and bewildering as in this part of the Waveney valley; hedges tend to run riot in East Suffolk, but nowhere are they so insubordinate as here. There seem to be no signposts, and confusion becomes consternation when the group of villages known as the South Elmhams and Ilketshalls is encountered for the first time. Within a mile or two of each other lie hamlets called South Elmham St. Cross or Sancroft, South Elmham St. James, South Elmham St. Peter, South Elmham St. Margaret, South Elmham St. Michael, Ilketshall St. Andrew, Ilketshall St. John, Ilketshall St. Lawrence, and Ilketshall St. Margaret. No one seems able to distinguish between the two St. Margarets and I have never come across anyone able to direct me to an individual one of these villages. Near the Saints, equally inaccessible, lying forlornly by a little stream, far from lane or path, is the gaunt, tumbled ruin of a stern Saxon building circumscribed by a dry moat and consequently known as Moat Minster. It is a rectangle of thick, flint walls interrupted by jagged gaps which might once have been arches or windows

The Waveney preserves its wild spirit, its aloofness from civilisation throughout its great length, even near the end of its course when it passes close to Lowestoft and to two of the most overcrowded, popular places on the east coast, Oulton Broad and Fritton Decoy, a long, irregularly shaped lake, thickly wooded to the water's edge like the romantic lochs of Scotland. An unknown writer described wildfowling on the lake thus in 1790:

Fowl and fish are very plentiful here, the pike and eels being very large. The duck, mallard and teal are in such plenty as is scarce to be conceived. They are taken in prodigious flocks at a time in the decoys. They send these fowl to London twice a week on horseback, from Michaelmas to Lady Day, and one decoy will furnish twenty dozen or more twice a week for the whole season.

The spoils of Fritton Decoy are no longer brought to London on horseback, but the wildfowl are as plentiful as ever. The decoy is an ancient device for snaring wildfowl. It consists of a series of hoops like gigantic croquet arches set one behind the other across the water for a distance of about eighty or ninety yards. These hoops are covered with netting and are some twenty feet wide at the mouth, narrowing down to about a yard at the smaller end, so that the appearance of the whole is not unlike a long conical butterfly net of immense proportions half sunk in the water. Tame ducks are placed at the mouth to attract the wildfowl. When a great flock has assembled, the decoy man and his dog drive them up to the narrow end where they are trapped.

The marshes fed by the Waveney beyond Hoxne are as bleak as any in East Anglia. The tiny villages scattered over

Estuary of the River Alde at Aldeburgh

that territory, some of them like Syleham lying deep in the morass, are often completely isolated in winter by floods. Then the river loses itself in a menacing stretch of steel-coloured water, the only traces of its course the blackened tops of stunted willows. The east wind whips the flood into sinister waves which sometimes bear with them the pitiful fragments of stye or hen coop, farm implements or domestic utensils. In a severe winter the flooded water meadows near Bungay and sometimes the river itself are frozen. On two occasions to my own knowledge it has been possible to skate from Bungay to Beccles, a most stimulating experience, for in frosty weather the landscape is even lovelier than in summer. Except for the level stretches on either side of the river's course, the country is less flat than the Cambridge-

shire fens and the dazzling expanse of whitened fields and trees is enlivened by low hills, whose outline, shaped by frozen scrub and bracken, looks slightly out of focus in the bright air. The great tower of Beccles broods over the frozen river. The red brick houses on the slope below with their uneven, snow-covered roofs and the quaint waterside buildings complete the obvious likeness of the scene to a Dutch or Flemish picture.

Suffolk's rivers tell the same story as her market towns, of former prosperity and slow decline. Once, all the seaward flowing rivers were navigable far inland and turned the attention of Suffolk's pastoral folk towards the coast. Bales of cloth were taken by river to the centres of Ipswich on the Orwell, Beccles on the Waveney, Woodbridge on the Deben, Framlingham on the

Alde and Halesworth on the Blythe, which were all in direct touch with the sea and the trade routes to Flanders and France. Most of the estuaries have been silted up through the centuries and only Ipswich remains a trading centre. The strange alteration in the character of the rivers, their gradual withdrawal from the outer world has contributed much to the aloof, dreamlike atmosphere of Suffolk. The same sense of the past persists along the banks of a shrunken river like the Alde at Framlingham or the Deben above Woodbridge as haunts the streets of Lavenham or Hadleigh. The Blythe especially, is full of phantoms of bygone times. Above Blythburgh this once busy waterway is now no more than a stream, difficult to follow, for the path is obstructed by giant thistles and vicious nettles, while hordes of insects cloud the air with irritating hum. But thousands of butterflies delight the eye, feasting on the mint and loosestrife by the water's edge, sometimes as many as five clinging to one plant. Very soon, just beyond a high-backed bridge, the remains of a lock, black and broken, are seen. The stream reaches Wenhaston Mill in its setting of brilliant hillocky meadows where black and white Friesian cattle enjoy the fat pasture, and then discloses a fantastic sight, a ruined lock with its rotting gates and chains still in position. The lock is choked by weeds and saplings above, and below it is lost in a mass of water milfoil, ivy-leaved pond-weed and the flowers of the arrowhead and the rush. Where the river has dwindled it has left behind a dense undergrowth of celery-leaved crowfoot, yellow cress, star-wort and golden dock. Farther on still are traces of another lock, a few mouldering timbers, then the water slips through a little plantation of alders and again there is the sombre spectacle of a ruined lock, this time a charred-looking cage-like object stranded in a wilderness of rushes. In Halesworth itself, which lies but a short distance from here, the course of the former river runs straight by a malthouse, an indication that barrels were once dispatched by water instead of by rail. Near the malthouse is an inn called the Wherry, a modern building now connected only by its name with the river. Inquiry reveals that a reed-thatched tavern, burnt down some twenty years ago, once stood on the site of the Wherry, right on a quayside, the lost harbour of Halesworth. A grass-grown basin is all that remains of the place where wherries were wont to come up to the brewery.

Ruined locks mark the course of streams which were once important rivers and deserted or decaying water and windmills often bring a melancholy note into the Suffolk scene. Some watermills, like the celebrated one at Flatford, are put to uses which have no connection with their original purpose, others are completely abandoned. At Bramfield a vast disintegrating watermill appears with its rent walls like a battlemented castle. Windmills are rapidly falling into disuse. The solemn sound of the sails sweeping round in the hush that always seems to lie about a mill is becoming rare in Suffolk. In the marshlands lying about the river estuaries windmills were formerly safeguards against flooding. At high tide when the surface of the rivers is above the level of the water in the dykes pumping is necessary and this work was always done by windmills. Steam has now largely taken their place and often the truncated tower is all that survives of this picturesque building once so characteristic of fen districts, a blackened finger pointing like so much else in Suffolk to the past.

7

THE COAST

Edward Fitzgerald once said, 'There is no sea like the Aldeburgh sea. It talks to me'. He was prejudiced, yet it is true that nowhere is the consciousness of contact with the sea greater than along the wild, lonely Suffolk shore. I feel that this springs from its unalterable character, for it has not changed since the Danes first raided East Anglia. Unlike the rest of the English coast, which has suffered more than the countryside from the jerry builder's lack of taste and scruple, the Suffolk shore is unspoiled. There is no coast road. Impenetrable marshes and heaths and innumerable mazy rivers, some of them flowing for miles parallel to the sea, make it impossible to follow the line of the beach. Between Lowestoft and Felixstowe, some fifty miles, there are only eight villages actually by the sea, and the eighteen solitary miles from Aldeburgh to Bawdsey are interrupted by not more than the handful of cottages known as Shingle Street.

The desolate beaches where nothing grows but coarse grass, the flat stretches of swamp, the reedy estuaries are the nesting places of thousands of birds. The piercing, plaintive notes of sea and marsh birds are familiar night sounds along the Suffolk shore. Sometimes in spring I have been awakened by the shrill whistle of great flocks of curlews flying to their breeding grounds in the north. And in autumn the widgeon arrive in their hundreds, flying at a tremendous height in the darkness, the air vibrating with the thin, whining sound of their wings. Very often the marshes are fringed by forests running right down to the sea's edge. An oak wood grows beside Easton Broad near Southwold. It is a silent, mysterious place. An overgrown path leads through the trees towards the sea. Through the trunks the glittering waters of the Broad and the straw-coloured ranks of rushes can be seen. Suddenly the gentle wood becomes a scene of waste and confusion. The earth looks as though it has been churned in battle, the green trees are become gaunt skeletons, some of gigantic size. Whitened by the salt spray they twist at strange angles or lie prone. Beyond them is an expanse of shingle and the mild, blue sea.

It is the sea, so bland, so serene and indolent on a fine day, which has wrought this destruction. In winter the shore is beseiged by monstrous waves. Sullenly, relentlessly driven by the gale, they crash and surge inland, while the fisherman stands helpless beside his little boats and the wildfowl move restlessly among the marshreeds. I have already mentioned some of the disasters brought about by coast erosion. The story of Dunwich has been related by everyone who has written about East Anglia. The harbours at Easton and Minsmere have been lost forever. Those at Orford and Bawdsey have been rendered almost useless. There is not a town or village on the Suffolk coast that is not the subject of a tragic tale. At Covehithe nothing remains of a once prosperous fishing community but a few cottages on top of the sandy cliffs and the ruins of a vast church, a great tower with the walls of aisle and chancel crumbling away. Within the nave of this immense skeleton a tiny, plain, modern church has been built. There is a parallel to this strange sight at Walberswick where a new church has been constructed within the ruins of the old. Massive piles have been driven into the shore to break the sea's onslaught, colossal pieces of timber at least two feet square, the beautiful pattern of the grain on them smoothed and polished by the fret of the water. A Southwold man told me that many of these piles had been cut from oaks that must have been growing in Suffolk for nearly a thousand years.

The Suffolk coast with its lonely beaches and hidden creeks was formerly the haunt of smugglers. In the eighteenth century the headquarters of a large body of Suffolk bootleggers was at Hadleigh. An account in the *Gentleman's Magazine* of 1750 describes how 120 horses and 100 smugglers worked throughout the summer of 1750 landing dry goods and tea at Sizewell Gap. They were finally caught and their leader John Harvey was found guilty at the Old Bailey and sentenced to transportation. Richard Cobbold in his celebrated *History of Margaret Catchpole, a Suffolk Girl*, writes vividly of the Suffolk smugglers and of the Preventive Service men whose lives were even more dangerous than those of the freebooters. Margaret Catchpole, who was a servant in the house of John Cobbold, an

Ipswich brewer, loved a smuggler from Felixstowe, Will Laud, and disguised herself as a sailor and stole her master's horse to follow her lover to London. Horse stealing was punishable by death, but Margaret was sentenced only to transportation for seven years. Before the penalty could be put into force, however, the girl broke out of her Ipswich prison, climbing over the spikes on the summit of the high wall, and joined Will on Sud-

Aldeburgh

bourne beach where a boat was waiting to carry them both to Holland. They were about to embark when the officers of the law came upon them. Margaret was retaken and Laud was shot dead by the coastguard. The girl was tried again and moved the court with her romantic story as well as by her intrepid bearing, so that the death sentence at first passed on her was reduced to transportation for life. Margaret was twenty-eight when she sailed for Australia. There she recovered from her ill-starred love and married a respectable settler at Windsor. But she never forgot Suffolk. To her friends at Ipswich she presented a lyre bird and to Richard Cobbold, rector of Wortham, she sent the story of her life. At the *Jolly Sailor* at Orford there can still be seen one of the original handbills offering £50 reward for the capture of Margaret Catchpole after

her escape from Ipswich gaol.

At either end of the Suffolk coastline there is a flourishing seaside town. Felixstowe is a pleasant enough place, but it does not enter into my view of Suffolk. Fortunately it has not harmed its immediate surroundings. Lowestoft, on the other hand, spreads too far. The flint-walled, red-roofed cottages of the old town have been engulfed by modern development. Still, its ancient fishing industry gives it an atmosphere of romance. All kinds of fish—turbot, sole, cod, plaice, skate, mackerel and herring—are landed daily at the Trawl Market. In autumn, when the industry is at its height, the largest fleet of herring drifters in England glides into Lowestoft harbour, and the Lowestoft wives, aided at that time of year by the 'Scottish lassies', wallow through the great heaps of fish, followed by the uncouth yelling of the fishermen across the docks.

Neither Felixstowe nor Lowestoft is truly Suffolk in spirit. The most characteristic of the places on the coast is perhaps Southwold, a bright, breezy little town of narrow streets, flint or old red brick cottages, and rows of small colour-washed houses giving on to pleasant greens which end abruptly by the steep, shingly beach. The lighthouse, with due regard for the devouring sea, has been built well back from the shore. Its smooth, startling white shape rises up from the heart of the streets, it shines out above the gravestones in the churchyard, and nowhere can one avoid the flash of its ruby eye. An old-fashioned advertisement for Elliman's Embrocation in the main street reminds us that Southwold is an agricultural as well as a seaside town, but the sense of the sea pervades every inch of the place. Spray is blown through the air, the smell of the sea is about all the houses, every road leads to the sea, and its mystery and magic are made tangible in the shape of old ships' figureheads languishing on doorsteps and in gardens.

From Southwold a path parallel to the sea runs by a dyke over a low, level marsh

Lowestoft

to the Blyth. The ferry across the river has broken down and if you would see Walberswick on the opposite bank you must wait upon the charity of an old sailor of uncertain temper or skirt the marsh and pass over the water at Blythburgh, a walk of nine miles. On the Southwold side of the Blyth, about a mile from the sea is a picturesque group of cottages and warehouses and the old Anchor Inn. Fishermen foregather there on a Saturday evening and sing part songs with many verses of their own invention. Their voices are so hearty, their words so jolly that the whine of the wind over the fen outside, the plundering sea and its tale of woe are quite forgotten. They continue their song even after closing time and the sound of it fills the keen night air as they make their way either on foot or on bicycles back to Southwold.

8

THE PAINTING OF SUFFOLK

Our vision of nature is often determined by art. We look at Monte Sainte Victoire through the eyes of Cézanne, the landscape round Aix en Provence is forever coloured by Van Gogh's view of it. Our conception of one part of the Suffolk countryside, the valley of the Stour, is largely decided by Constable's impassioned interpretation. It is difficult for anyone to look at those rich summer meadows with a regard fresh enough to re-create them. Gainsborough's rendering of his native scenes, on the other hand, has scarcely influenced our idea of

41

Suffolk, but his few early landscapes, the most poetical and inspired if not the most accomplished of his works, show us that there are some aspects of the scene which Constable did not attempt.

Thomas Gainsborough was born at Sudbury, in 1727, the son of a woollen manufacturer. It is impossible to visit the little town without becoming aware of Gainsborough's origin. His name flashes out from notice boards, from the front of cinema, café, shop, school and hotel, and his statue is prominent in the market place. Though so much advertisement hardly accords with the short period of his life Gainsborough spent in his birthplace, it is in one sense just that his connections with Sudbury should be so insistently proclaimed, for it was here when quite an untaught boy that the passion for landscape, his true passion, despite all his portraits, first came upon him. He said that as a boy he had drawn all the ancient tree trunks and picturesque details of the country near his home, many of his sketches the prize of truancy from school. These absences Thomas owed to his skill in forging his father's handwriting in letters to the headmaster asking for leave.

Among the landscapes in oil from this early Sudbury period is *Cornard Wood*, now in the National Gallery. It is a picture of an oak forest where woodcutters are at work and where an opening at the end of a winding path yields a distant glimpse of a church on the summit of a gentle hill. To the right is a small stagnant pond. It is a simple and direct statement of the theme, yet it contains all the poetry and magic of Suffolk in spring; it catches and imprisons in a mood of lyrical reverie the fresh morning, the sparkling yellow-green foliage and the impressive cloud formations flashing over the landscape their sudden contrasts of light and shade.

Gainsborough's talents seem to have attracted the attention of the local gentry, but when commissioned to paint their portraits it was of Suffolk as much as of them he thought, for he painted them as incidents in their native landscape. Of these delightful compositions the best known are *Mr. and Mrs. Brown of Tunstall*, a village not far from Woodbridge, and *Mr. and Mrs. Andrews*. In *Mr. and Mrs. Brown of Tunstall* the sharply emphasised figures are set on the right of a long landscape. The strongly accented clouds, the group of farm buildings on a slope above a pond, the leafless trees against the sky, the pines at the water's edge, the oak behind the figures, though not the recognisable portrait of an actual place, reflecting as they do a personal, poetic mood, could be nowhere but in Suffolk. *Mr. and Mrs. Andrews* is an even more striking interpretation of the Suffolk landscape. The lady sits beneath a broad oak tree and her husband with gun and dog leans upon the arm of the ornamental iron seat. To the right and far away behind them stretches the Suffolk countryside, an early autumn landscape with stubble and stooks of corn in the foreground; beyond, sheep in a meadow, oakwoods dark under the shadow of piling clouds and far away a patch of cornfield shining almost white in a ray of sun. It is a fresh, almost impressionistic painting of a scene just outside Sudbury expressing all the tranquility, the extraordinary stillness and loneliness which is the essence of the landscape in Suffolk.

Gainsborough was never, alas! to develop to the full his genius for landscape painting. Portraiture was the only avenue which opened to him and he was soon engulfed by the fashionable world. By 1752 he was in Ipswich, and though he made many sketches along the banks of the Orwell, so that Constable half a century later fancied he could see Gainsborough 'in every hedge and hollow tree' near Ipswich, in his paintings the figure began to predominate and landscape was gradually translated into the generalised formula for foliage and sky which is characteristic of his mature work. They are ideal landscapes which have no connection with Suffolk or even with England. At Ipswich, Gainsborough made influential friends, Joshua Kirby who later introduced him to the King and was thus responsible for the painter's conversation piece of the Roya Family, and Philip Thicknesse, Governor of Landguard Fort, who lured the painter to Bath and the patronage of society. Gainsborough knew and painted Clive, Burke, Pitt, Sheridan and Garrick, Sarah Siddons, Mrs. Robinson, dukes, duchesses and princes. He became famous and prosperous. Never again did he return to the solitary fields and woods of his native place. But in one of his letters there is a suggestion that they were not absent from his thoughts and that landscape was still his passion.

I'm sick of Portraits and wish very much to take my viol da gamba and walk off to some sweet village, where I can paint landskips and enjoy the fag-end of life in quietness and ease. But these fine ladies and their tea-drinkings, dancings, husband huntings, etc., etc., will fob me of the last ten years, and I fear miss getting husbands, too. But we can say nothing to these things, you know Jackson, we must jogg on and be content with the jingling of the bells, only damn it I hate a dust, the kicking up a dust, and being confined in harness to follow the track whilst others ride in the waggon, under cover, stretching their legs in the straw at ease, and gazing at green trees and blue skies without half my *Taste*. That's damned hard.

The peaceful farms and cottages, the few miles along the valley of the Stour between Manningtree and Nayland have become world famous as 'Constable's Country'; through the painter's interpretation this strip of land has come to represent more than any other place in England all that we know and love in the English landscape. Constable, like Gainsborough, could not sell his landscapes, but as he was not entirely without means he was able to devote a great part of his life to the study and painting of his native countryside. He was born on June 11th, 1776, at East Bergholt in a house near the church which no longer exists. The straggling village above the Stour, once a centre of the woollen industry, retains almost unaltered its original aspect with its few large, isolated houses, yellow plastered cottages clustered round its several greens

and its great church with the tower unfinished so that the bells cannot be suspended there but hang instead in a curious wooden cage in the churchyard. Constable's father owned watermills at Flatford and Dedham and two windmills in the neighbourhood of East Bergholt. He wished to make a miller of his son, too, and for about a year after he left the grammar school at Dedham, Constable worked in his father's mills. The time was not wholly lost to him as a painter. It was his duty as a windmiller, just as it was his inclination as a painter, to watch every change in the sky with peculiar interest, and he put his acquaintance with the machinery of wind and watermills to good use. His younger brother once said, 'When I look at a mill painted by John, I see that it will go round'.

Even as a schoolboy Constable was devoted to painting, and he early made friends with the only man in the village who had any feeling for art, John Dunthorne, a plumber and glazier who lived in a cottage near the gate of Golding Constable's house. In his company Constable spent all his leisure painting landscapes from nature. His native scenery from the first moved him more than any other subject. 'Painting with me is but another word for feeling,' he wrote years later to his friend, Archdeacon Fisher, 'and I associate my careless boyhood with all that lies on the banks of the Stour; those scenes made me a painter and I am grateful.'

In 1799, after his father had at last consented to his becoming a painter, Constable entered the Royal Academy Schools and in 1802 his name appeared for the first time in the catalogue of the annual Academy exhibition. From then onwards, London, eventually Hampstead, became his headquarters. But Suffolk was never far from his thoughts. His letters from London are full of longing for the woods and water-meadows of his boyhood. 'I pine after dear Suffolk,' he writes, 'I am sighing for the country,' or 'I am still looking towards Suffolk where I hope to pass the greater part of the summer . . . You know I have always succeeded best with my native scenes. They have always charmed me and they always will.' And whenever he was able to leave the heat and clamour of the city he hastened to East Bergholt and its neighbourhood. Only a few weeks before his death he was eagerly proposing a visit to Suffolk with his sailor son, Charles. The Suffolk landscape was the constant theme of his work. The more picturesque aspect of other counties did not move him. 'As to meeting you in these grand scenes,' he wrote once to Leslie, 'remember the great were not made for me nor I for the great; things are better as they are. My limited and abstracted art is to be found under every hedge and in every lane.' When a journey to Paris was proposed, Constable's reply was, 'I hope not to go to Paris as long as I live'. This may seem narrow-minded, violently insular, but the feeling that urged Constable to paint only what he knew and loved best was true. Travelling could scarcely have benefited one whose art was based on the continual study of the same passionately loved scenes under every change of atmosphere. Constable's greatness was derived from his exclusive devotion to the country of his boyhood.

He was the first to paint directly from nature out of doors—the first impressionist. But his originality was unrecognised in his own country. Except for his friend, Archdeacon Fisher, no one understood what he was about. He was only grudgingly admitted to the Royal Academy after embittering delays, at the age of fifty-three. By the time he was forty he had scarcely sold a landscape, though he had been sending in to the Academy for fourteen years. The dramatic story of how a French art dealer saw *The Haywain* and included it with twenty-four smaller works in the Paris Salon exhibition of 1824 is well known. The French painters were enthusiastic, Constable's influence on Delacroix and Géricault was decisive and *The Haywain* was awarded a gold medal. But Constable had little pleasure from this.

'Think of the lovely valleys and peaceful farmhouses of Suffolk forming part of an exhibition to amuse the gay Parisians,' he remarked apprehensively. He could not read French, he overlooked the penetration of the French critics and never attempted to follow up his success.

It was Constable's avowed aim to reproduce nature as closely as possible. And every sketch and large composition Constable made of Suffolk is in one sense an almost exact statement of the visible facts of the situation. Every one of his small studies shows an intensely observed moment in the landscape, they transfix those elusive and unimaginable qualities which in nature distinguish any particular moment from all others. Suffolk depends for its chief splendours upon the contrast of light and shade and it is natural that Constable's work should be based on chiaroscuro. He paints the church of Stoke-by-Nayland, brilliant and dramatic against the background of a gathering storm, the summer rain and shafts of light breaking over gleaners in an upland field, a pink house against the pearly light of evening, he paints a watermill surrounded by thick foliage and pines tossed by the wind and lurid in a sudden gleam of light, and the porch of East Bergholt church, rich and sombre amongst dark trees on a dull, late summer afternoon.

A visitor to 'Constable's Country' will be startled by the resemblance of some of these scenes to the pictures. The road from East Bergholt to Willy Lott's house and Flatford Mill passes the subject of *The Cornfield*. Nature has been astonishingly reproduced in the picture, though the trees on the left of the painting have now been felled and the view of Dedham church in the background cannot actually be seen from this point. A lane branches off to the right, at once recognisable as the scene of the sketch in the National Gallery called *A Country Lane*; the stream, the steep, tangled banks thick with cowparsley, campion and ragged robin, the trees on either side intertwining their branches overhead were painted by Constable

Gainsborough Street, Sudbury

towards sunset. The trunks are black against the light, the red, evening glow pierces the foliage and falls on the path. At the end of the lane is the subject of *The Haywain* unchanged, except that Constable's distant view of meadows is now obscured by trees and that the green solitudes are often now disturbed by busloads of sightseers and streams of motorists and cyclists whose company diminishes the pleasures of contemplation. Flatford Mill, which Constable painted from the back, was presented to the nation by Mr. Parkington of Ipswich, and has been turned into artists' studios.

It was Constable's habit to paint full size sketches of his six-foot canvases such as *The Haywain* and *The Leaping Horse*. The so-called sketches were made for his own satisfaction, the finished versions for exhibition to a public who would not accept the full impact of his powerful vision. The final version of a picture like *The Haywain* shows the calm, uneventful face Suffolk might show to a casual visitor. In the great sketches for this picture and for *The Leaping Horse* the countryside is revealed in all the intensity which characterise its more dramatic moments. Many of the sightseers at Flatford might well be bewildered as they contemplated these canvases. In the thick impasto, the impetuous brushstrokes, there is no such photographic resemblance as the prosaic eye might seek. There is no detail in the sketches. It is impossible to pick out a tree and to find its counterpart in nature. Piled up, agitated masses of cloud, trees and figures lose their separate identity, caught up in the glitter of light. All the fluctuating interchanges and interactions between the various objects of the scene, which in certain lights and at certain moments give such significance to the unpretentious landscape of Suffolk, Constable has interpreted. And his interpretation is meaningful because his passion for nature is balanced by his understanding of picture making. Claude, whose landscapes bear only the remotest relation to reality, was not for nothing the master Constable most admired. Constable combines to a degree unsurpassed, the freshness of the actual scene with all the essentials of architecture, tone, volume and mass. It is not necessary to know Suffolk to appreciate Constable's work, but those who share his love of this part of the country must always be moved by the realisation that the essential starting point of his painting is the Suffolk landscape and that the result is something unmistakably Suffolk in spirit.

9

SOME LITERARY ASSOCIATIONS

MANY famous men and women of letters have been associated with Suffolk. There can be no pretence here of writing of more than one or two of them. Jocelyn of Brakelond, Friar Bungay, named after his native place and the subject of one of Robert Greene's most popular plays, Marie Louise Ramée, born at Bury and best known as Ouida, the rustic poet Robert Bloomfield, author of the *Farmer's Boy*, Gray's visits to Blundeston, Lamb's stay at Fornham can be no more than mentioned. Even the choice story of Chateaubriand's love affair with his pupil, Miss Ives of Bungay, cannot be related in all its delightful detail. Chateaubriand, known in Suffolk as Mr. Shatterbrains, and his pupil were mutually attracted and Miss Ives concluded that it was only her master's lack of means that prevented a proposal. Her mother took a

like view of the matter and one day suggested to the amorous Frenchman that he should marry her daughter and inherit the Ives' property. Chateaubriand himself describes his reactions: 'I threw myself at Mrs. Ives feet and covered her hands with my kisses and my tears. She stretched out her hand to pull the bell-rope. "Stop," I cried, "I am a married man!" She fell back, fainting.'

Edward Fitzgerald, George Crabbe and George Borrow claim more earnest attention. Edward Fitzgerald did not immortalise Suffolk in his work like Constable, Crabbe and Gainsborough, but in one way he had a stronger connection with the county than any of these. Except for brief visits to France and London in his youth and his three years at Cambridge he never left Suffolk during the whole of his seventy-four years. So it is his life there, which he so charmingly describes in his letters, and his strange yet lovable personality which shall be my concern here. He was born at Bredfield House, an imposing Jacobean mansion about half an hour's walk from Woodbridge, painted white, fronted with Dutch gables and set in a cowslip park sloping down to the drowsy valley of the river Deben. The green of the bordering woodlands, the flash of the tidal waters can be seen from the windows of the house. Fitzgerald always had pleasant recollections of his Bredfield home, though he feared more than loved his beautiful, imperious mother and hid in the shrubbery whenever he saw her large yellow coach and four black horses coming up the drive. He took pleasure in his father's fine collection of pictures, furniture and china, but did not in the least share his other interests—sport, politics and society. He prefered to wander about the Suffolk lanes making friends with all the queerest characters of the neighbourhood.

Fitzgerald returned from Cambridge where he had formed lasting friendships with Thackeray, Frederick and Alfred Tennyson, Frank Edgeworth, brother of the novelist, and James Spedding, to settle in Suffolk for good and to indulge his passion for the arts. His family meanwhile had removed first to Wherstead near Ipswich, then to Boulge Hall, a Queen Anne house, again near Woodbridge. Beside one of its park gates was a quaint little one-storeyed thatched cottage. In the spring of 1837, when the cowslips and primroses were in full bloom, Fitzgerald took up residence in this cottage, using the room on the right of the entrance as his study and filling it with his books, a bust of Shakespeare, a piano, music, pipes and walkingsticks. To attend to his needs there were John Faiers and his wife, the former a Waterloo veteran, the latter 'a snuffy but vain old woman, with very red arms, who wore beside other vanities, an enormous bonnet, full of flowers'. His companions were a cat, a dog and his parrot, Beauty Bob. Here, clad usually in his dressing gown he wrote, painted, played Handel and Mozart and entertained his odd medley of friends. The most congenial of his immediate circle was perhaps the Rev. George Crabbe, son of the poet and called by Fitzgerald 'The Radiator' on account of the gleams of wit and wisdom he so freely emitted. This was his answer to an invitation to dine at Boulge:

> As sure as a gun
> I'll be in at the fun
> For I'm the old Vicar
> As sticks to his liquor;
> And smokes a cigar
> Like a jolly Jack Tar;
> I've no time for more
> For the post's at the door;
> But I'll be there by seven
> And stay till eleven,
> For Boulge is my Heaven!

It was during this period at Boulge Cottage that Fitzgerald met Edward Byles Cowell, afterwards Professor of Sanskrit at Cambridge, who first inspired him with the idea of translating the *Rubaiyat of Omar Khayyam*. At this time he seems to have entered with far more zest than he ever showed in earlier or later life into such social pleasures as Boulge and Bredfield afforded. Sometimes he helped Caroline Crabbe, daughter

of the vicar, to teach in the Bredfield village school, while on Sundays he rendered a similar service to Lucy Barton in the Sunday school. Caroline seems to have inspired him with more than friendship, but it was Lucy whom more by accident than design he came to marry. Lucy was the daughter of Bernard Barton, the Quaker poet of Woodbridge, a close friend of Fitzgerald's. He promised the dying Barton that Lucy should be provided for, and she understood this to imply marriage. Fitzgerald was too embarrassed and perplexed, too gentle to resist, and his 'pleasant, Robinson Crusoe existence' at Boulge Cottage was thus brought to an end. The union was disastrous. As a conventional husband attending social functions and dinner parties Fitzgerald was, of course, a miserable failure. Lucy was equally incapable of adapting herself to his eccentricities. In 1860 they parted and Fitzgerald returned to his old life of careless indolence, this time in lodgings on the Market Hill in Woodbridge. The waxen bust (Lady, of course) in the hairdresser's shop opposite, which so entertained him as it mechanically revolved, was still in the window last summer, though the barber had forgotten to wind her up.

For thirteen years, despite an income which would have enabled him to live in luxury, Fitzgerald remained in this room, where there was so little space for his pictures and all his knick-knacks that it looked 'like a back shop in Wardour Street'. He had always loved the Deben and now he became not only fond of sailing but of the company and dialect of seamen. 'I am happiest going in my little boat,' he wrote, 'round the coast to Aldboro', with some Bottled Porter and some Bread and Cheese, and some good rough soul who works the Boat and chews his Tobacco in peace. An Aldboro' sailor, talking of my Boat said: "She go like a wiolin, she do." What a pretty Conceit, is it not, as the Bow slides over the Strings in a liquid Tune? Another man was talking yesterday of a great Storm: "and, in a moment, all as calm as a Clock".' He paid frequent visits to Lowestoft, usually travelling by sea and nearly always staying at one or another of the two southernmost houses, Nos. 11 and 12 of Marine Terrace. But it is the cliffs, the beach, the harbour jetties and the fishermen's quarters that seem haunted by that pensive figure. He hated 'respectable' South Lowestoft, 'our ugly Lowestoft' as he called it. It is difficult to imagine what he would think of it now. He was especially fond of the North beach, its net-chambers and curing sheds. There he would chat with the fishermen who were mending their nets and whose nicknames were all known to him, Lew Colby, Dickymilk Colby and old Brawtoe; and he came to know the fishermen's talk and lore so well that he made a glossary of Suffolk nautical terms and colloquialisms, most of which are still used today. He included beside the list of words his own diverting notes, of which the following is an example:

HORRYWAUR. Fifty pounds to the philologer who will guess this riddle without looking to the end for its solution. When first I knew Lowestoft, some forty years ago, the herring luggers (which then lay on the beach, when not at sea), very many of them, bore testimony to Wesley's visits to the place, and his influence on the people. Besides the common family and familiar names, such as William, Sarah Jane, Two Friends, Brothers and such like, there were the Ebenezer, Barzillai, Salem, and many more Old Testament names, besides the Faith, Hope, and Charity, etc., from later Revelation. A few vessels bore names in profane story—such as the Shannon (which, by the bye, still reigns) after Sir Philip Broke's victory; there was even a William Tell (no longer reigning), whose effigies, drest in an English sailor's white ducks and blue jacket, pointed at the wind with a pistol from the masthead. *That* was about the furthest reach of legendary and historic lore. But *now* the schoolmaster has been at sea, as well as abroad, and gone herring-driving. Bless me! there's now a 'Nil Desperandum', a 'Dum Spiro Spero' and last, not least, a 'Meum and Tuum'; though in the latter case it was very properly represented to the owners that the phrase being Latin should properly run 'Meum et Tuum'. Then even the detested 'Parley-vous' has come into request; and you may hear of a

'scrunk' of luggers very gravely enumerated in such order as the following. 'Let me see—there was the Young William, the Chanticleer, the Quee Vive (Qui Vive), the Saucy Polly, the Hosanna and the Horrywaur'. Of the latter I could get no explanation, until one day it flashed upon me when I saw sailing out among the fleet, the 'Au Revoir', belonging to a very good fellow who goes, as I believe his father went before him under the name of Dicky-milk.

In 1863 Fitzgerald had built for himself a small schooner yacht, the *Scandal*, 'named after the main staple of Woodbridge,' and captained by Thomas Newson of Felixstowe, who always carried his head on one side reminding his master of a magpie looking into a quart pot. He was succeeded by Joseph Fletcher of Lowestoft, who became one of Fitzgerald's dearest friends. The friendship between the uncultured fisherman and the gentle dilettante, now past middle age, must necessarily have been one-sided, and Fitzgerald's descriptions of the beloved 'Posh' are extravagant to say the least. He is represented as 'a man of the finest Saxon type, with a complexion *vif, mâle et flamboyant*, blue eyes, a nose less than Roman, more than Greek, and strictly auburn hair that any woman might sigh to possess,' and further, 'a man of simplicity of soul, justice of thought, tenderness of nature, a gentleman of nature's grandest type. Altogether the greatest man I have known'. The appearance of Fitzgerald himself at this time was in touching contrast to this dazzling creature. According to Thomas Wright he 'was above the medium height, but at sixty, though still robust and nimble, had begun to stoop. His face, bronzed by the sun and sea air had a melancholy, pensive or dreamy cast; he had pale blue eyes, bushy brows, a large nose, a deep upper lip, a firmly closed mouth, and a dimple in the chin. Save for a fringe of grey hair above the ears he was bald and like all the Fitzgeralds he wagged his head as he walked'. His attire was slovenly. Abroad he wore a time-beaten tall hat, carried on the back of his head, a carelessly tied black scarf round his neck and in cold weather a large green and black plaid shawl, which often trailed on the ground. His dress never varied, even on board. While Posh had complete charge of navigation, Fitzgerald, in his singular costume, would stretch full length on the deck, smoking and reading Greek and Latin, often aloud.

However incongruous, Fitzgerald and Posh remained together for ten years. Posh even, according to Fitzgerald, became rather literary and composed at least two songs, one of which shows such rich imagination and feeling that, judging from authentic reports of the skipper's reaction to his master's verse, the reader is tempted to doubt Fitzgerald's word:

I once loved a boy of my own, bonny boy,
I loved him I vow and protest,
I loved him so well, so very, very well
That I built him a nest on my breast.
The thoughts of green laurel wept over the plain
Like one that was troubled in mind,
So I hollared and juped and played on my flute,
But no bonny boy could I find.
I looked up high and I looked down low
When the sun shone so bright on its charms,
And there did I espy my own bonny boy
Close confined in another girl's arms.
My own bonny boy he is gone far away,
He has left me this wide world to tarry,
But if he loves another better than me,
Shall for his sweet sake I not marry?

Posh's love of the bottle was eventually too much even for Fitzgerald and the relationship came to an end.

In 1872 Fitzgerald's landlord, Sharman Berry, became engaged to marry a widow and his tenant who was far from pleased at the news remarked that 'old Berry would now have to be called Old Gooseberry'. The injudicious witticism was repeated to the widow and its perpetrator ejected from his lodgings. Berry was sad to part with him but the widow was determined. When Berry ascended to Fitzgerald's room to announce the decision, she stationed herself at the foot of the stairs

calling out, 'Be firm, Berry! Remind him of what he called you!'

After a few months in the house next door, Fitzgerald moved to his last Suffolk home, Little Grange, an old farmhouse on a by-road almost at Melton leading to Bredfield and Dallinghoo. Here Charles Keene, whose acquaintance Fitzgerald had made at Dunwich, was a frequent visitor. He often walked in the garden of Little Grange playing the bagpipes, while his host sat for hours at the organ, playing on until nothing of him was to be seen in the

Eye

gloom but a dim outline and the pendulous shape of the ever present shawl. Alfred Tennyson and his son visited Little Grange, in 1876, and soon after leaving Suffolk Tennyson recalled his stay in the dedication to *Tiresias*

Old Fitz, who from your suburb grange,
Where once I tarried for a while,
Glance at the wheeling Orb of change
And greet it with a kindly smile . . .

Fitzgerald died in 1883, not at Little Grange, but whilst on a visit to Crabbe's grandson at Merton on the Norfolk border. He arrived there on June 13th tired but cheerful, and after sauntering for a while in the garden went early to bed. Next morning he was found to have died quietly in the night. His body was brought home to Suffolk and buried in Boulge churchyard.

George Borrow and Edward Fitzgerald

were both disposed to enjoy the luxury of a simple life, both given to exaggerating the good qualities and homely wisdom of humble companions, both eccentric and unconventional. Yet they never became friends. They met at the house of William Bodham Donne, in Westgate Street, Bury, in October 1856. But Borrow repelled Fitzgerald 'by his masterful manner and uncertain temper'. They were in fact entirely dissimilar in character and person. Borrow was tall, like Fitzgerald, but his carriage was very upright. He had thick hair which had turned white when he was no more than twenty, a strangely smooth pink face, an acquiline nose and small, piercing, dark eyes. His temperament was changeable, fierce and stormy, untamed by all his travels and adventures. There are many stories of his behaviour when he lost his temper. One of the victims of his rudeness was Agnes Strickland, who was introduced to Borrow at a reception at Bury St. Edmunds, then the centre of a literary circle. She began before long to praise his books and asked him whether she might send him a copy of her *Queens of England*. We can scarcely imagine her embarrassment when she received the reply: 'For God's sake don't, madam; I should not know where to put them or what to do with them'.

By the time George Borrow settled in Suffolk, in 1840, he was thirty-seven years of age. The fantastic adventures, the life of vagrance related in his books were already behind him. He was master of more than forty languages, had wandered all over England and Wales, explored every corner of Europe and the greater part of Asia, he had been to Russia to translate the New Testament into Manchu and had spent four perilous years in Spain working on behalf of the Bible Society. He was born in Norfolk, but he never returned there after his father's death in 1824 and Suffolk has more claim to him, for it was on the shores of Oulton Broad that he spent the longest stationary period of his life and it was there, leading an existence of unaccustomed mildness, that he wrote

The Zingali and *The Bible in Spain, Lavengro* and *The Romany Rye*, and the heroine of the last two works, Isopel Berners, was born in Suffolk at the Great House, Long Melford.

In Borrow's day, Oulton Cottage was a small, solitary house separated from the waterside by a sloping lawn and sheltered by rugged fir trees, one or two of which yet survive. In the garden was a long, octagonal summerhouse which Borrow made into a study. He describes how whilst writing he would be constantly distracted from his work by the pleasures of nature. On a fine day he could not resist mounting his Arab stallion, Sidi Habismilk, and riding for days together over the heaths and through the green lanes of Suffolk; He would sometimes catch pike in the Broad or lie for hours in the sun, quite forgetful of *The Bible in Spain*. The restlessness which had prompted the wanderings of his youth never left him; he often rode twenty miles before breakfast. And after an attack of the 'Horrors' (the terrible melancholia to which he was all his life subject) he would walk fifty miles in a day. Sometimes he would say to his wife at breakfast 'I am going for a walk,' and he would disappear not for a couple of hours, but for as long as three months on end, taking nothing with him but the clothes he was wearing.

Borrow's unpredictable ambition whilst at Oulton was to become a magistrate so that he could adjucate upon the delinquencies of his neighbours, but he gave little evidence of possessing the cool judgment which would commend him to the Lord Lieutenant of the county. So irritable was his disposition that he would quarrel over the slightest trivialities. He carried on an interminable feud with the rector of Oulton because of the frequent fights between their respective dogs, even threatening to launch an appeal to the magistrates and a complaint to the Bishops. Once in acknowledging a note from the rector, Borrow regretted that circumstances over which he had no control would occasionally bring them under the same roof. 'That roof, however, is the roof of the House of God and the prayers of the Church of England are wholesome from whatever mouth they proceed.' If Borrow, thought he had in any way been injured he would pillory in print those who appeared to have wronged him. He once rode his horse into the hall of Dr. Ray's house at Lowestoft because his coachman in turning a corner sharply had almost grazed the flank of Sidi Habismilk. His fury against the railway contractor who came to construct a railway between Reedham and Lowestoft which happened to cross his estate is more understandable and was perpetuated in the appendix to *The Romany Rye*. He frightened children by glaring at them when he encountered them in his walks, and chased on horseback some boys who had called after him uncomplimentary names.

Borrow always remained on good terms with the gipsies. He had a real and deep kinship with them; they were the symbols of that romantic, mysterious excitement for which his imagination was always striving. His Romany friends often camped on a waste track of land near Oulton Cottage and it was in his summer house that Borrow received for the last time the famous Jasper Petulengro, whose acquaintance he had made many years before in the green lane near Norman Cross. Perhaps it was only the pride of this most self conscious of men and a too tender regard for the world's opinion which prevented him from throwing in his lot entirely with the roving folk. He would certainly have felt more at ease with them than with his neighbours at Oulton. He was far too angular to conform to their characterless self-complacency. They hardly ever cared to call on him for no one could be sure of a friendly reception. One of his latest visitors, the rector of Lowestoft, happened to ask him how old he was. Borrow at once became very angry, exclaiming, 'Sir, I tell my age to no man'. Then in high dudgeon he retired to his summer house and began his last composition with the words: 'Never talk to people about their age'. He died in 1881 and was buried not at Oulton, but in Brompton cemetery, London, beside his wife.

Among the villas of modern Oulton, Borrow would scarcely recognise the site of his cottage. The quiet, winding lane in which it stood has been replaced by a busy motor road, the view over the Broad is ruined. Nothing here recalls that tall figure with the thick, white hair and the terrifying eyes. Only the marshlands stretching away down the Waveney valley, soothing the eye with their wild, spacious monotony, silent but for the wail of the lapwing, still speak of that solitary man who wandered so far but sought in vain for happiness.

Chelsworth

Constable devoted his life to the interpretation of the Suffolk landscape. George Crabbe also spent his energies in fashioning a picture of Suffolk, not only of the countryside but of the people. Both alike aimed at reproducing as closely as possible the scenes before them, both created something more dramatic, more significant than nature. Here the resemblance ends, for Constable was concerned only with the aspect of valley and meadow, seen usually whether in storm or fair weather, in the fullness of summer, while Crabbe describes not only the desolate coast landscape of his native Aldeburgh, but the grim, sordid lives of the people. The 'amenity and elegance' which Constable mentions in a letter as being typical of Suffolk are replaced in Crabbe's poetry by the horrors of the Poor House and the depressing poverty of the fishing community. No one has portrayed the Suffolk coast and marshlands more vividly than Crabbe or conveyed with more feeling the tragedy wrought by the encroachment of the sea. The following lines depict as faithfully today as in the eighteenth century much of the country lying inland from Aldeburgh:

> On either side
> Is level fen, a prospect wild and wide
> With dykes on either hand by ocean's self supplied;
> Far on the right the distant sea is seen
> And salt the springs that feed the marsh between;
> Beneath an ancient bridge the straitened flood
> Rolls through its sloping banks of slimy mud;
> Near it a sunken boat resists the tide.

But Crabbe's descriptions are seldom more than aids to the interpretation of character, a background to the sadness and squalor which the poet knew from his own experience.

He was born in 1754 at Aldeburgh and grew up amid scenes of wretchedness. He gives a realistic picture of the little town; piles of refuse lay in the dreary back streets where starved dogs, pigs and chickens looked for food and sick children wailed unattended. Crabbe's home life provided him with some of his most moving scenes of domestic distress. Crabbe's father seems to have turned his hand to anything which would provide him with a bare living, from schoolmaster to warehouse keeper and collector of salt duties. He was a soured, violent, gloomy man, overfond of the bottle, contemptuous of his son's studious disposition and of his incapacity to share in the management of the fishing boat in which he sometimes took his children to sea. 'That boy,' he would say, 'must be a fool. John and Bob and Will are all of some use about a boat, but what will that thing ever be good for?' Yet he realised that the solitary, fanciful

boy was gifted, and at a far greater expense than his circumstances warranted he sent him to school at Bungay and at Stowmarket and decided that he would make a surgeon of him. Some time elapsed before he could be apprenticed and George was given employment, bitterly distasteful to him, in his father's warehouse at Slaughden. At length he was accepted as an apprentice by a so-called doctor at Wickhambrook. It is doubtful whether the conditions of his life were at all improved or whether he learned here anything of the medical profession, for he was set to work in the fields and his bed-fellow was a ploughboy. After three miserable years he was transferred to a surgeon at Woodbridge. That move decided the whole course of Crabbe's life. It was at Woodbridge that he first began to write and there that he fell in love with Sarah Elmy, his future wife. Sarah's time was divided between her home at Beccles and the house of a rich uncle at Parham, a large, lonely, moated farm called Ducking Hall. In his accounts of Uncle Tovell's farm Crabbe gives one of the best extant descriptions of life in a yeoman farmer's home in the eighteenth century, in particular of the gigantic meals of which the labourers, tinkers and ratcatchers used to partake in the kitchen. These orgies so disgusted the delicate Sarah that:

> She could not breathe, but with a heavy sigh,
> Reign'd the fair neck and shut the offended eye,
> She minced the sanguine flesh in frustums fine
> And wondered much to see the creatures dine.

In *The Lover's Journey* Crabbe relates how he rode up the coast from Aldeburgh to visit Sarah at Beccles. Hardly anything in the landscape has changed since he made the journey one hundred and fifty years ago.

At Woodbridge, Crabbe published his first long poem *Inebrity*. Then towards the end of 1775 he returned to Aldeburgh to find his home in such a state it seemed impossible he would be able to complete his education. His father had succumbed entirely to drink, his mother was fatally ill and terrified by her husband's violent temper and brutal conduct. There was no money and George was compelled until his mother's death to return to the much loathed Slaughden Quay. As soon as he could he escaped to London to finish his apprenticeship and set up in Aldeburgh as a doctor on his own account. His medical career was a hopeless failure. He had to contend for a share of Aldeburgh's patronage with a clever, active practitioner and he was ruined by his passion for botany. His ignorant patients, seeing him come home day after day with handfuls of weeds from the shore and the marsh dykes, put him down as a dangerous quack. Crabbe himself brought this unsatisfactory state of affairs to an end in 1780. He was by this time determined to be a poet and set off for London with but three pounds and a small case of surgical instruments.

After two years of poverty, struggle and the rejection of his work by all but one publisher, this shy, awkward countryman succeeded in establishing himself. He numbered amongst his friends some of the most distinguished and influential men of his day, among them Burke, Fox and Sir Joshua Reynolds. But he longed to return to Suffolk, and after qualifying himself as a deacon he was at his own request licensed as curate to the rector of his native town. This was mistaken, for the people of Aldeburgh—

.... A wild amphibious race
With sullen woe displayed on every face,
Who far from civil arts and social fly
And scowl at strangers with suspicious eye,

had not forgotten the dock labourer of Slaughden, the unsuccessful doctor and the debaucheries of Crabbe's father. So Crabbe eventually became curate of the two small villages, Great Glemham and Sweffling. It is pleasant to think of his gentle life there, bowling along the lanes in a one-horse chaise, gathering wild flowers and reading aloud to his family in the evenings. He was beloved by his parishioners, although some of his ways were rather strange. He was often blunt in his address. On tithe day he would say to his congregation: 'Gentlemen, I must have some money,' and on one or two occasions when evening drew on before he had finished his sermon he remarked abruptly: 'Upon my word I cannot see; I must give you the rest when we meet again'. During this time Crabbe wrote *The Borough* and *The Parish Register*, also three novels, which, when his family condemned them, he cheerfully burnt.

In 1805, Crabbe was called to Muston in Leicestershire and only once again did he revisit his native Suffolk scenes. This was shortly after his wife's death, which had greatly affected him. He spent a day rambling in the neighbourhood of Parham and Glemham, everywhere reminded of the happy years he had spent with Sarah. After his death his son found in his notebook the following lines which he had composed during that solitary walk:

Yes, I behold again the place
The seat of joy, the source of pain;
It brings in view the form, the face
That I must never see again.

The night-bird's song that sweetly floats
On this soft gloom—this balmy air,
Brings to the mind her sweeter notes
That I again must never hear.

Lo! yonder shines that window's light,
My guide, my token heretofore;
And now again it shines as bright,
When those dear eyes can shine no more.

Then hurry from this place away!
It gives not now the bliss it gave;
For Death has made its charm his prey,
And joy is buried in her grave.

Crabbe's most impressive work, *The Borough*, is full of interest to every native of Suffolk; it is of special importance today, for the tragic character of Peter Grimes, the brutal fisherman suspected of the murder of his apprentices, inspired the first opera of Benjamin Britten, himself a Suffolk man, born at Lowestoft.

10

EPILOGUE

IT has not been possible in an essay of such moderate length to name more than a few of the places and objects of interest in Suffolk, to call attention to more than a small number of the romantic and curious remains of antiquity or to give more than a passing glance at the beauties of landscape. I can only hope that from the little I have said the seeing eye will discover for itself all the delights I have left unmentioned. In describing the silent, old-fashioned villages, the moated halls, the great churches, the lonely heaths and marshes of this most unspoiled of counties I have tried to convey a sense of the isolation, wildness and decay which to me make up the picture of Suffolk. I have given a personal impression rather than a factual account. Such an account would refer to the establishment of such industries as the sugar beet factories, the pepper and spice mills, the processing of agricultural products, the manufacture of agricultural implements; it would touch upon the increase of educational facilities and of social amenities. Accurate information on all such points has been supplied by authorities far more competent to speak of these matters than I. A clear, concise bird's-eye view of the whole situation is given in *The Suffolk Planning Survey* by T. E. Oxenbury, published at Ipswich, in 1946.

While the growth of urban industry in Suffolk has so far scarcely changed the visual aspect of the county, the revival of agriculture during and since the war noticeably offsets the general sensation of decline. In the thirties, agriculture was in no better condition than the country crafts which were being eliminated by mechanical mass production. It was not uncommon in Suffolk to see barns with their thatch stoved in and farmhouses with the plaster ripped off their walls in dismal patches. The sheepflocks were disappearing, more and more arable fields were going down to grass each year. This sad state is not entirely altered. There is still a lack of interest in the craft of farming, which bodes ill for an agricultural county. Haystacks are often so badly made that they are blown down in the first gale, and where a hedger has been at work, the scene usually resembles a battlefield: the branches are jagged, raw, hacked off and split, the whole hedge is shapeless. The youth of every village still sets its face whenever possible towards the nearest town. But with the timely help of the prisoners of war, with improved rates of pay and the possibility of better conditions, the farmers are slowly shaking off their apathy, the land is once more under control, the farms repaired and repainted. Perhaps the day is not far off when we may happily experience a return to the Suffolk described by William Cobbett, who exclaimed at seeing

the land in such a beautiful state—the barns and every thing about the homesteads so snug; the stocks of turnips so abundant; the sheep and cattle in such fine order; the wheat all drilled; the ploughman so expert; the furrows if a quarter of a mile long as straight as a line, and laid as truly as with a level; in short, here is everything to delight the eye, and to make the people proud of their county; and this is the case throughout the whole county. I have always found the Suffolk farmers great boasters of their superiority over others, and I must say it is **not without reason.**

Brandon

INDEX

The page numbers of illustrations are shown by italics

Acton, 27, *75*
Alde, River, 7, 15, 33, 35, 38, *82*
Aldeburgh, 10, 38, 39, 51, 52, 53
Allen, Admiral, 18
Alpheton, 7, 28
Ancient House, Ipswich, 10, *61*
Applethwaite, Bridget, 30
Avon, River, 32

Barking, 12
Barton, Bernard, 47
Barton, Lucy, 47
Barton Mills, 32
Bawdsey, 39
Beccles, 37, 52
Bedingfield, Sir H., 16
Berners, Isopel, 50
Berry, Sharman, 49
Bigod, Hugh, 15
Bigod, Roger, 15
Blaise, Saint, 27
Bloomfield, Robert, 46
Blundeston, 46
Blyth, River, 38, 41
Blythburgh, 23, 41, *72*
Borrow, George, 46, 49-51
Bouchier Family, 8
Boulge Hall, 47
Box, River, 7
Boxted Hall, 9
Brakelond, Jocelyn of, 14, 20, 46
Bramfield, 30, 38
Bramfield Oak, 16
Brandon, 30, 31
Breckland, 16, 30, 34, *76*
Bredfield House, *84*
Brent Eleigh, 32, 59, *60*
Brett, River, 32
Breydon Water, 12, 33
Bristol, Fourth Earl of, 8
Britten, Benjamin, 53
Brown, Andrew, 28
Bungay, 15, 35, 37, 52
    Castle, 15, *63*
Bungay, Friar, 46
Bures, 13
Bures, Sir Robert de, 46
Burgh Castle, 10, 12, 33, 35
Burke, Edmund, 43, 53
Bury St. Edmunds, 10, 13, 14, 20,
    21, 30, 50
    Abbey, 13-14, *62*
Butley, 7

Carlyle, Thomas, 20
Catchpole, Margaret, 39-40
Catherine, Saint, 27
Cavendish, 23, *69*
Cedd, Saint, 13
Cezanne, 41
Charles I, 16, 22
Charles II, 16, 18
Chateaubriand, F. R., 46
Christopher, Saint, 28
Chelsworth, 19
Clare, 20, *66*, *67*
Claude, 46
Claydon, 8
Clive, Robert, 43
Clopton Family, 26
Cobbett, William, 10, 54
Cobbold, Richard, 39
Coddenham, 23
Constable, John, 23, 32, 41, 43-46,
    51
Cordell, Sir William, 16, 18
Covehithe, 39
Cowell, Edward Byles, 47
Crabbe, Caroline, 47
Crabbe, George, 46, 51-53
Crabbe, Rev. George, 47

Dallinghoo, 49
Darcy Family, 8
Deben, River, 7, 34, 35, 37, 46, 47,
    82, *83*
Dedham, 43
De la Pole, Michael, 36
Dennington, 23, 27
De Ruyter, 18
Donne, William Bodham, 50
Dorothy, Saint, 28
Dove, River, 7
Dowsing, William, 16
Ducking Hall, 52
Dunthorne, John, 43
Dunwich, 10, 39, 49

Earl Soham, 19
East Bergholt, 43, 44, *70*
Easton Broad, 39
Edgeworth, Frank, 46
Edmund, King, 13-14, 28
Edward VI, 15
Edward the Confessor, 16

Elizabeth, Countess of Oxford, 23
Elizabeth, Queen, 16, 21
Elmy, Sarah, 52, 53
Elveden, 30
Ely Cathedral, 34
Euston, 30
Evelyn, John, 18

Faiers, John, 47
Felix, Saint, 13
Felixstowe, 10, 39, 40, 48
Fisher, Archdeacon, 43
Fitzgerald, Edward, 38, 46-50
    House, *84*
Flatford, 38, 43, 44, 45, *78*, *84*
Flaxman, 9
Fletcher, "Posh", 48-49
Flint Knapping, 30-32, *74-75*
Flushwork, 23
Fornham All Saints, 23
Fornham St. Genevieve, 15, 46
Fox, Charles James, 53
Framlingham, 15, 16, 37, 38
    Castle, 15, *63*
Fressingfield, 26
Fritton Decoy, 36
Frostenden, 7-8

Gage Family, 8
Gainsborough, Thomas, 9, 12,
    41-43, 46
    Birthplace, *86*
Gardiner, Bishop, 16
Garrick, David, 43
Gipping, 23
    River, 34, 35
Glem, River, 7
Glemham, Sir Thomas, 7
Glemsford, 23
Gray, Thomas, 46
Great Bealings, 27
Great Glemham, 34, 53
Greene, Robert, 46
Grimes Graves, Norfolk, 31
Grundisburgh, 26, *71*

Hadleigh, 16, 20, 22, 32, 38, 39
Halesworth, 38
Hartest, 19-20, 30, *61*
Harvey, John, 31

Hasketon Church, 73
Hawstead Place, 16
Helmingham, 16
Hengrave Hall, 8, 14
Hogarth, William, 9
Holton, 79
Howard, Henry, Earl of Surrey, 15
Howard, Sir William, 23
Hoxne, 13, 35, 36
Hunsdon, 15
Huntingfield, 16

Icklingham, 31
Ickworth House, 8-9
Ilketshalls, the, 36
Ipswich, 10, 12, 16, 21, 22, 34, 37, 38, 40, 42, 45, 47, 54, 57, 61

James I, 16
Jermingham, Sir Henry, 15

Kauffmann, Angelica, 9
Keene, Charles, 49
Kentwell Hall, Long Melford, 8, 26
Kersey, 19, 22, 32, 60, 64
Kirby, Joshua, 42
Kytson Family, 8

Lamb, Henry, 46
Lark, River, 7, 14, 32
Laud, Will, 40
Langham, 83
Laurence, Saint, 28
Lavenham, 19, 21, 23, 27, 28, 38, 58, 67, 69
   Guildhall, 19
   Wool Hall, 19
   Church, 70
Lawshall, 32
Lindsey, 19, 22, 32
Lingheath Common, 31
Linnet, River, 7
Little Glemham, 7, 34
Little Grange, 49
Little Ouse, River, 31, 34, 35, 80-81
Long Melford, 16, 18-19, 21, 22, 23-26, 66
   Hall, 18
   Church, 70, 72
Lott, Willy, 44
Lowestoft, 10, 18, 39, 40, 48, 51, 85
Lydgate, John, 14, 26

Manningtree, 43
Mary Tudor, 15-16
Merton, 49
Mettingham Castle, 36
Mildenhall, 23, 26
   Treasure, 12
Minsmere, 7, 39

Moat Minster, 36
Mockbeggar Hall, 8
Monewden, 19
Monks Eleigh, 19, 59
Montgomerie, Sir Thomas, 23
Muston, Leicestershire, 53

Nayland, 43
Newmarket, 16, 18
Newson, C., 27
Newson, Thomas, 48
Norman Cross, 51

Orford, 37, 39
Orwell, River, 7, 12, 34, 37
Ouida, 46
Oulton Broad, 36, 50, 51
Oxenbury, T. E., 54

Pakefield, 10
Parham, 34, 52, 53
Parkington, T. R., 45
Parge work, 10, 20
Pepys, Samuel, 18
Petulengro, Jasper, 51
Pitt, William, 43
Pygot, Richard, 23

Redwald, King, 13
Reedham, 51
Reynolds, Sir Joshua, 9, 53
Richmond, G., 28
Robinson, Mrs., 43
Roos Hall, 36
Rougham, 16
Rushbrooke Hall, 16

Santon Downham, 34, 80-81
Sandwich, Earl of, 18
Saxtead, 34
Severn, River, 32
Shelly, 16
Sheridan, R. B., 43
Shingle Street, 39
Siddons, Sarah, 43
Sizewell Gap, 39
Slaughden Quay, 53
Smallbridge Hall, 16
Sole Bay, Battle of, 18
Somerleyton, 28
South Elmhams, the, 36
Southwold, 18, 28, 39, 40-41, 85, 86, 88
Spedding, James, 46
Spryng, Thomas, 19
Stanstead, 23, 30, 72
Stephen, King, 15
Stoke-by-Nayland, 23, 34, 44
Stour, River, 7, 32, 34, 35, 43
Stowmarket, 21, 22, 52
Strickland, Agnes, 50
Sudbury, 21, 22, 42
   Archdeacon of, 31

Sutton Hoo Burial Ship, 13, 68
Sweffling, 34, 53
Sweyn, King, 14
Syleham, 37

Talbot, Elizabeth, 23
Taylor, Dr. Rowland, 16
Tennyson, Frederick, 46
Tennyson, Lord, 46, 49
Thackeray, W. M., 46
Thetford Warren, 30
Thicknesse, Philip, 43
Thornham Magna, 77
Thornham Parva Retable, 27
Tilney, Elizabeth, 23
Tollemache Family, 16

Utber, Admiral, 18

Van Dyck, 16
Van Ghent, Admiral, 18
Van Gogh, 41
Velazquez, 9
Vere, John de, 19

Walberswick, 39, 75
Waldringfield, 34
Walpole, 68
Watkinson, Elizabeth, 30
Watkinson, William, 30
Waveney, River, 7, 12, 23, 33, 35-37, 51, 78
Wenhaston, 12, 38
   Doom, 28
Westhall, 27
West Row, 12
West Stow Hall, 74
Wherstead, 47
Wickhambrook, 12, 52
Windsor, Australia, 40
Wingfield Castle, 36
Wissington Church, 69
Wolsey, Cardinal, 12
Wolsey's Gate, Ipswich, 10
Woodbridge, 34, 37, 46, 47, 48, 52, 59, 83, 87
Woollen Trade, 20-22
Woolpit, 23, 74
Wortham, 40
Wrentham, 20
Wright, Thomas, 48
Wyatt, Sir Thomas, 15
Wye, River, 32

Yare, River, 12
Young, Arthur, 22

Zoffany, J., 9

A farm near Lavenham
Edwin Smith

A farm near Woodbridge
Crown copyright

The church and village green
of Monk's Eleigh
Leonard & Marjorie Gayton

The Hall, Brent Eleigh
A. F. Kersting

59

View across cornfields towards Kersey
Crown copyright

Oxlips growing in a wood near Bury St. Edmunds
The Times

The seventeenth-century Congregational chapel at Hartest
Edwin Smith

The plasterwork figure of Europe below one of the first floor windows of
the Ancient House, Ipswich. *A. F. Kersting*

The Dog and Partridge Inn and St. Mary's Church, Bury St. Edmunds,
looking towards Angel Hill. *Crown copyright*

The Butter Market, Bury St. Edmunds
Crown copyright

Framlingham Castle
Crown copyright

Bungay Castle
A. F. Kersting

The village
street
and ford,
Kersey
*Crown
copyright*

A house decorated with pargeting at Clare
National Buildings Record

Part of the village green, the Black Lion Inn and the church, **Long Melford**
Leonard & Marjorie Gayton

Tudor Houses, Lavenham
Leonard & Marjorie Gayton

Fourteenth-century houses, Lavenham
Leonard & Marjorie Gayton

LEFT TOP
Blythburgh Church,
built in the fifteenth century,
is distinguished by
the openwork parapet
of its south aisle,
and by its
elaborate flint work
A. F. Kersting

LEFT CENTRE
An early nineteenth-century
tombstone carved with a
recognisable image
of the village church,
in Stanstead churchyard
Edwin Smith

LEFT BOTTOM
A fourteenth-century
alabaster plaque of
the Adoration of the Magi,
in the wall of the north aisle,
Long Melford Church
A. F. Kersting

RIGHT
Hasketon Church,
near Woodbridge.
An unusual feature of the
Norman tower is the
octagonal shape
of the upper part
A. F. Kersting

Elizabethan wall paintings in the gatehouse of West Stow Hall in Breckland, representing four of the seven ages of man
H. J. Smith

LEFT
An example of flushwork, a pattern worked in dressed flints between two of the clerestory windows at Woolpit Church
H. J. Smith

RIGHT
A flintknapper at the mouth of a pit near Brandon.
Paul Popper

Freshly quarried flint
Paul Popper

The knapper in the foreground is engaged in the first stage of dressing a flint, 'quartering' it. The man behind is fitting a flint into a gun
Paul Popper

The font, Walberswick
A. F. Kersting

A poppy head, Acton Church
Edwin Smith

LEFT TOP
The pine trees and
solitary wastes of
Breckland
The Times

LEFT BOTTOM
Stone Curlews on
Breckland
Eric J. Hosking

RIGHT TOP
A saddle maker's shop,
Clare
Edwin Smith

RIGHT BOTTOM
The mill, Thornham Magna
Hallam Ashley

77

The Waveney in flood at Homersfield, near Bungay *Hallam Ashley*

OPPOSITE A mill at Holton, near Halesworth *Crown copyright*

A thatched cottage on the Stour at Flatford *Crown copyright*

The Alde, near Iken. *Crown copyright*
ON PAGES *80-81* A stanch at Santon Downham on the Little Ouse *Hallam Ashley*
The Deben at Waldringfield. *Crown copyright*

A tide mill on the Deben at Woodbridge. *E. Lovell*

A water-mill at Langham. *H. W. Fincham*

84

LEFT TOP
The Sole Bay
Inn, Southwold
Edwin Smith

LEFT BOTTOM
Gainsborough's
birthplace,
Sudbury
F. A. Girling

RIGHT
The old
steelyard and
the Bell Inn,
Woodbridge
Crown copyright

86

A Suffolk Punch. *Sport & General*

An advertisement in the main street, Southwold. *Edwin Smith*

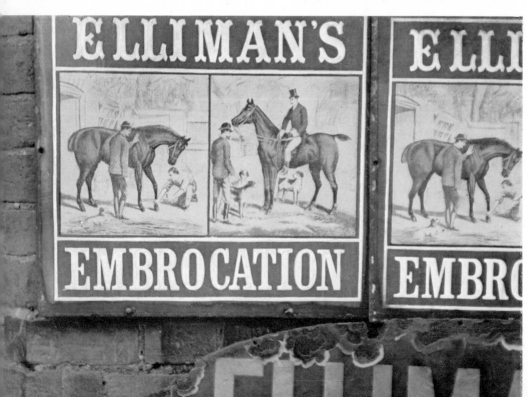